Manchester Ghosts
New Hampshire's Haunted City

Renee Mallett

Renee Mallett

Schiffer Publishing Ltd

4880 Lower Valley Road Atglen, Pennsylvania 19310

Dedication

This book is for my Grandma, who never let a Christmas pass without there being a book of ghost stories under the tree for me.

Published by Schiffer Publishing Ltd.
4880 Lower Valley Road
Atglen, PA 19310
Phone: (610) 593-1777; Fax: (610) 593-2002
E-mail: Info@schifferbooks.com

For the largest selection of fine reference books on this and related subjects,
please visit our web site at **www.schifferbooks.com**
We are always looking for people to write books on new and related subjects. If
you have an idea for a book please contact us at the above address.

This book may be purchased from the publisher.
Include $3.95 for shipping.
Please try your bookstore first.
You may write for a free catalog.

In Europe, Schiffer books are distributed by
Bushwood Books
6 Marksbury Ave.
Kew Gardens
Surrey TW9 4JF England
Phone: 44 (0) 20 8392-8585; Fax: 44 (0) 20 8392-9876
E-mail: info@bushwoodbooks.co.uk
Website: www.bushwoodbooks.co.uk
Free postage in the U.K., Europe; air mail at cost.

Copyright © 2007 by Renee Mallett
Library of Congress Control Number: 2007920917

Designed by Mark David Bowyer
Type set in UniversityRoman Bd BT / NewBaskerville BT

ISBN: 0-978-7643-2650-9
Printed in China

Contents

Disclaimer 4

Acknowledgments 5

Introduction 8

Great Chief Passaconaway 16

Elliot Hospital 23

Saint Josephs Middle School 28

The Murder of Jonas L. Parker 32

The R. G. Sullivan Building 38

The Grandmotherly Ghost 43

A Not So Helpful Spirit 46

Avery 51

The Horror on Hanover Street 55

Hesser College 65

An Apartment Building on Beech Street 76

The Palace Theatre 80

The Home Coming 85

The River Road Jogger 89

Saint Anselm College 93

Samuel 104

Strange Happenings on Rock Rimmon 107

Man's Best Friend 118

The Youth Detention Center 127

The Party That Never Ends 134

Valley Street Cemetery 137

Haunted New Hampshire 152

A Conversation with Manchester's Ghost Hunter 163

Spirit Photography 101 169

Bibliography and Website Resources 174

Disclaimer

This is a book of real-life ghost stories and other unexplainable occurrences. The stories are based on true accounts told to me by the people who have experienced the hauntings themselves. Some of the cases are quite famous and can be found on the internet as well. Many of the stories, like all great ghost stories, have an element of local legend or folklore to them, and they walk the thin line between fact and fiction.

This book could not exist without the generosity of the people who shared their stories with me and, as the old saying goes, many of the names have been changed to protect the identity of the people involved.

Please keep in mind that all of the places written about here are real places that offer the opportunity to you, the reader, to go and see for yourself. The places described are those of business, education, and private homes. Before visiting any haunted site, remember that the living people in these places deserve respect first and foremost. That is why exact house numbers, and, usually, not even street names, are given for the private homes that are written about in this book. Never trespass on other peoples' property; always get permission to visit a site before you decide to go ghost hunting. There are a great many companies that you can find in travel books, online, and in the yellow pages, that give tours of haunted places. These ghost tours are an ideal, safe, and legal way to experience haunted places and ghostly phenomena yourself, usually for a modest admission fee and without taking on the added risk of a trespassing charge.

Acknowledgments

No book is ever solely created by one person, and this book benefited from the help and support of many people whom I'd like to take a moment to thank. First, I need to thank my family and friends, who in the most polite way possible, listened to my nervous breakdowns and never complained about all the social events and family gatherings I missed while interviewing, photographing, and writing *Manchester Ghosts*. My parents and my in-laws all did a lot of babysitting so I could complete this book—much appreciation to them in particular!

A great many thanks to Lisa Weinberger, Dinah Roseberry and Staci Layne Wilson—all of them top notch editors (Dinah at Schiffer, Lisa at Pearlywrites, and Staci Layne Wilson is the horror guide at About. com, among easily half a dozen other publications). They are all incredible writers themselves, with a few books between them, that I recommend heartily to readers. These three woman gave me breaks into this difficult world of writing, and have all helped guide me through the process of writing a book, among other projects. It has often been said that it's not what you know, but who you know, and I'm lucky to know such outstanding ladies.

I am very much indebted to the two great librarians in my life, Tom Neenan and Tina Barnes, who not only lent their helping hands to *Manchester Ghosts*, but also their sympathetic ears. They helped not just with the research, but gave their support as friends. The staff at the Chester Public Library, and the wonderful librarian in the New Hampshire room at the Manchester Public Library, were excellent sources as well. The one thing I've found to always be true in life, is that if you want to know about, or how to do anything, a librarian can usually point you in the direction you need to go.

The paranormal investigators at Ghost Quest were an enormous help; their founder, Raven Duclos, told me stories of their exploits, let me page through their ghost photographs, and listen to the many electronic voice phenomena (EVPs) that they have taken over the years. They were able to add a great deal to the stories I had tracked down myself, and told me quite a few more that I had never heard before. If you are interested in electronic voice phenomena, spirit photography, and hauntings, this group's general website, www.ghostquest.org, will be of interest to you. So, big thanks to Raven Duclos, Beckah Boyd, Katie Boyd, and Fred Turner for their generosity and for their intrepidness in facing the things that go bump in the night.

Krystal Garrison is the photographer who did my author photograph for this book. She is an extremely talented and an award-winning artist, all on top of being a smart sassy lady. Check out her website, www.KrystalGarrison.com, to see more of her work.

And last, but certainly not least, I owe a great deal of thanks to all the people who sat down with me, or took the time to email me, to tell me their stories, all seeming to begin with: "I never use to believed in ghosts, but then this one day, the strangest thing happened to me . . ."

Introduction

New England probably ranks up there as one of the most haunted areas in the world. It has the mythology and folklore of the Native Americans, some of the oldest colleges in the country, abandoned centuries-old farmhouses, small harbor towns that have lasted through terrible storms and hard times, the superstitions of the seafaring fishermen, lonely old lighthouses, fog filled graveyards, spooky bed and breakfasts, and all the hysteria and paranoia of the witch-hunting years. Actually, when you consider the rich and diverse history of the New England states, the question isn't so much *why* is New England so haunted, but more like, why isn't it even *more* haunted then it already is?!

When you talk about ghosts in New England, some stories and images come right to mind. The many grizzled, ghostly sea captains in Maine, perhaps. Or the much documented and talked about hauntings at the Lizzie Borden Bed and Breakfast in Fall River, Massachusetts, where the infamous and unsolved murders of a well-respected businessman and his wife took place. The one thing most New England towns don't seem to lack is reputable haunted houses, and ghosts have become a big tourist attraction for many towns. Check out any good sized city in the Northeastern states and you are sure to find at least one, and more often, several, places that offer tours of their towns' ghostly attractions.

When people start sharing their favorite stories around the campfire, you'll find one state that usually gets left out—New Hampshire. There aren't many New Hampshire hauntings that come immediately to mind. But don't start thinking that this means that there aren't any spirits in the Granite state! In fact, it's a surprise for most people, but New Hampshire is the site of the first true, recorded, and authenticated haunting in all of the United States.

While Maine may be a close contender for the title of earliest known haunting, so far, the prize seems to belong to New Hampshire. Joseph Citro, a folklorist and author of such books as *Weird New England* and *Cursed in New England: Stories of Damned Yankees,* tracked down a well-documented case of possible poltergeist activity that took place in New Hampshire all the way back in 1682. The story occurs in New Castle, which even today, is known for being the smallest town in the state. Located on one larger island and several smaller ones, the village of New Castle covers just .8 square miles.

In 1682, New Castle was just as small, if not smaller, and there was no way the Walton family could keep the extraordinary things happening to them a secret for very long. One terrible morning, the family woke up to hear a strange sound from outside. It sounded, vaguely, like rain, but much, much heavier. Running outside, they realized the frightening truth. The house wasn't getting rained on, the house was being pelted with stones!

Some as small as pebbles, others large enough to leave a good sized bruise if they struck you, this flurry of rocks appeared to be falling directly out of the sky. What made this freakish weather phenomena even more unusual was that the storm of stones was directed solely at the Walton homestead—the rest of New Castle was enjoying a warm spring day, without a cloud in the sky. Neighbors were soon drawn by the noise, and everyone searched in vain, trying to find the source of the outburst.

Odder still, when the Waltons went back inside their home to get away from the sharp sting of rocks, they discovered that it was raining rocks inside, as well as out. The floor of the house was already covered with several inches of rock. The family knew the stones couldn't be coming through the windows, as they were all closed and locked.

The Waltons continued to be plagued by falling rocks for some months. There seemed to be no way for anyone in the family to get away from it. When they fled the house and took up residence with a friend, the stones followed them. When they gave up and moved back into the house, the rocks ceased falling at their friend's house. Not only was it impossible to imagine how the rocks were coming to fall on the Waltons, but they couldn't figure out where anyone would even get so many stones to begin with.

At one point, the head of the Walton household, George Walton himself, gathered up some of the stones after a particularly heavy rockfall, marked them with paint, and locked them away in the house. Within a few days the stones had removed themselves from where they were hidden, and once again, rained down on the Walton home. George saw the stones he'd painted fall back out of the sky with his own two eyes.

As you can imagine, the weather problems that followed the family was big news back in 1682—just as it would be today. The family was very well thought of in town, and the thought of them trying to pull off such an elaborate hoax was unthinkable. On top of their outstanding reputations, much of the Walton family troubles were witnessed by Richard Chamberlain, who was secretary of the colony of New Hampshire at the time. He was an adamant supporter of the family and the authenticity of the bizarre occurrences happening to them. With such a prestigious witness on scene, it was not long before scientists came from all over the country, and all over the world, to either find a rational explanation for the problem or to debunk the Waltons outright. Every last one of them would leave confused and angry when, one after another, their experiments failed to produce results. The scientists could not come up with even one theory that the rocks didn't defy. The fall of rocks was, and remains to be, a mystery.

After some time, the rain of stones stopped, and didn't start again. Eventually, an old woman, who was a neighbor of the Waltons, would be accused of using witchcraft against the family. The woman was, perhaps, lucky in the fact that the events at the Walton household occurred ten years before the witch-hunting craze struck in Salem, or she may have met with a terrible fate for the townspeople's suspicions against her.

Knowing that New Hampshire has such a long history of unexplainable events, it should come as no surprise that Manchester, the largest city in the state, as well as being the largest city in northern New England, has more then its fair share of haunted places. While the stories may not go back as far as that of the Walton family's stone-falling nuisance, some of these tales trace back to the days from before there even *was* a city in the spot where Manchester stands today.

The original residents of Manchester were the Penacook Indians, and there are a few local legends that say that some of those early residents live on in the city to this day. Many of Manchester's schools are home to ghosts, as well as the expected haunted houses, and sometimes, encounters with former residents who just can't seem to move on from the places they loved so much in life. Part of the reason why Manchester might be so haunted, may be because of how closely the city of today resembles what it *was* in the past. Unlike many other urban areas, in Manchester, old buildings are not forgotten or torn down. The mills and factories that once made the city the rival of the textile city of the same name in England, are still being used to this day. They no longer produce shoes, cigars, or material—now the spaces have been renovated into ultra-modern, highly appealing office and retail spaces.

But it doesn't seem as though many of the old factory workers can tell the difference. There have been many reported paranormal encounters between the buildings' current residents and the people that worked there hundreds of years ago. Part of what makes Manchester the city it is, is the way that its past and present sometimes collide—with frightening results!

You'll find more then just frightening specters in this volume of true-life ghost encounters. Also, there are some sentimental tales of kind old spirits watching over their family after passing on, the story of an old Vaudeville actor who has returned to the stage at the Palace theater, even a handful of stories about dogs and cats that stay loyal to their masters—even in death!

Manchester is a modern cosmopolitan city, conveniently located just fifty miles north of Boston, and home to a minor-league baseball team, a dozen colleges, and the 10,000-seat Verizon Wireless Arena. The city may have been voted the number one city in America by *Money Magazine*, but it has always had its share of quirks. It is the only city in the country whose main street ends in two dead ends. One of the worst fires in Manchester's history was caused by 2,000 drunken, rioting firemen who were visiting the city for a conference. It was the location of the first credit union in the United States. Famous Manchester residents include the comedian Adam Sandler and "Commodore" George Washington Morrison Nutt, who was declared the smallest man in the world by P. T. Barnum.

One of the many statues dotting the landscape of Manchester. This one is the Victory Monument; its inscription reads, "In honor of the men of Manchester who gave their services in the war which preserved the union of the states and secured equal rights to all under the constitution. This monument is built by a grateful city."

Manchester's ghosts are no less eccentric then its living residents. Jogging fanatics, prank-playing kids, and the friendly soul, known as Avery—who hangs around a local subshop—all contribute to Manchester's colorful history, as well as the unique culture still visible today.

One City Hall Plaza, completed in 1846, after fire claimed the original City Hall in 1844. A later addition to this building (unseen in photo) makes it the tallest building in northern New England.

Great Chief Passaconaway

The earliest residents of Manchester were the Penacook Indians, who were part of the great Algonquin tribe. During the height of their civilization, the Penacooks occupied the northeastern part of Massachusetts through southeastern New Hampshire, and up through Maine with a population of just over 12,000 people in more then thirty villages. However, by the time white settlers had made their way north to the spot where they would later create the city of Manchester, those numbers had been reduced to a mere 2,500 (due to typhus and smallpox outbreaks). Not to mention an eight-year-long war with the neighboring Micmac tribes, over the fur trade with French settlers in Maine. Despite their battles with nearby native people, the Penacooks were said to be peaceful corn farmers and, surprisingly enough, considering the cool winters of the northeast, tobacco growers. The local tribe of Penacooks centered their land and migrations around Amoskeag Falls, which would later become the starting point of Manchester's textile mills. The Penacooks, of course, didn't honor the spot for its prime manufacturing location as the later Amoskeag Cotton and Wool Company would. Instead, Amoskeag Falls was revered for its plentitude of fish. So many, in fact, that the tribe not only kept themselves fed with a high protein diet of fish, but they used the fish as fertilizer for the corn and tobacco crops as well.

At the time when the first white explorers began to trickle into New Hampshire, the Penacooks were led by the great chief Passaconaway. In the native tongue, Passaconaway meant 'Child of the bear,' and the name was fitting for the great chief. Passaconaway made his name, firstly, as a great hero in the wars the Penacooks fought against the Micmacs. After becoming the leader of his tribe, Passaconaway would become known as much for his wisdom, as for his prowess in battle. Even during life, though, there was always talk about the supernatural powers of Chief Passaconaway. The stories the natives told about him, that survive to this day, tell of his ability to foretell the future, accurately predict the weather, and how he could restore green life to dead plants. The Penacooks said that he could handle snakes without being bitten, and that he could even cause water to freeze with just a touch of his hand. Even today, the inscription on the statue of Passaconaway, in Lowell's Edson Cemetery, commemorating the great leader, says that the man lived to be an unlikely 122 years old.

"Like the budding of spring leaves, they come in great numbers," Passaconaway told his people, when the first white settlements began to grow into prosperous towns further down the Merrimack, and it became harder and harder to find game while hunting.

Passaconaway was, perhaps, among the first of the Native American chiefs to realize that life, as his people had known it for countless generations, could not continue on in the face of this influx of new people. Although there is little actual proof of this and we do know that Passaconaway did not convert himself, legend says that it was Passaconaway who invited a missionary named John Elliott to come to Amoskeag Falls and preach the Christian religion to the tribe.

As the town of Manchester, called Derryfield at this point, began to grow along the Merrimack River, the fishing grew worse and worse. It became harder and harder for the Penacooks to gather enough food to feed their whole tribe. Passaconaway was growing old, and he knew that his time as leader was over, but he wanted to see his people prosper and thrive. He called together the people of his tribe and gave a rousing speech, pleading with them to make peace with the white settlers and adapt to the new world that was dawning around them. Passaconaway then handed the leadership of the tribe over to his son.

"Peace," he implored his people, "peace is the only hope of our race."

Soon after this speech, Passaconaway sensed that his time had come. The old Indian warrior took his canoe down to Lake Massabesic and started to paddle towards Loon Island. It was a place that was said to hold memories of happier times for the aging chief, and is one of several small islands that dot the surface of the lake to this day.

The day was bright and warm, but as Chief Passaconaway rowed towards the small island, the sky grew black and the waves on the lake started to surge higher and higher, threatening to tip over the small craft. The whole thing was so unusual that the tribe started to gather along the shore to see if they could figure out what was going on. Lightning flashed endlessly, blinding the crowd, and the first small drops of rain began to strike the surface of the lake. Somehow, everyone gathered could sense that their holy spirit, Kichtou Manitou, was the one causing the upheaval.

Lake Massabesic, as seen from Auburn New Hampshire; this popular fishing spot is also the center of an ancient haunting.

Out in the water, in just a homemade canoe, Passaconaway threw down his paddle and stood up in the flailing boat, raising his hands towards the darkening sky. No one could hear what he said over the noise of the storm, but he appeared to be screaming at the sky. Legend says that suddenly there was a flash of light, far brighter then that of ordinary lightning. In an instant, the dark cloud had passed and the sun peaked out its rays again. As quickly as it had darkened, the day once more became bright and calm. But when the tribe looked for Passaconaway, both he and his canoe were gone. By some means, in the brief instant of light, man and craft had vaporized into nothingness.

Today, Lake Massabesic supplies water for nearly 125,000 area residents. It has even become a popular tourist spot. Because the lake is used for drinking water, swimming is prohibited and boating is carefully regulated. The New Hampshire Department of Fish and Game keep the lake well stocked with trout, and it is one of the best places in the northeast to catch small-mouth bass and yellow perch. But some visitors to the area catch more then just a scale-tipping fish while at Lake Massabesic— some catch a glimpse of the great chief Passaconaway as well.

The ghost of Chief Passaconaway manifests itself in several ways. In the more then 200 years since he died, many people have reported seeing an incredibly old man, his face heavily wrinkled and careworn, but with a peaceful smile, wrapped in a homespun blanket in a rough hewn canoe on the waters of Lake Massabesic. They say that if you take your eyes off of him for even the briefest of moments, when you look again, he has disappeared without a trace, much as Passaconaway was said to have disappeared on the day he lost his life. Oftentimes, when looking out towards Loon Island, you can see a rainbow in the shape of a circle in the sky above the island. Legend says that this is a sign of the Native American warrior watching over the lands his tribe once owned.

Some people swear that seeing Chief Passaconaway is a warning of bad weather to come, and that if he is seen more often then usual in the summer months, it means that there is an especially harsh winter to come.

Sailboats on Lake Massabesic.

The spirit doesn't seem to bother the fish, though. Local fisherman swear that the best fishing in New Hampshire is right off the shores of Loon Island, in the spots where Great Chief Passaconaway's ghost is seen most often.

Welcome to Lake Massabesic . . . watch out for ghosts.

Elliot Hospital

Elliot Hospital is a 296-bed healthcare facility that has been serving Manchester (and all of southern New Hampshire) medical needs since they opened their doors in 1890. The hospital is known for its trauma unit, it's cancer facilities, and for the dedication and caring of its staff. One of the hospitals workers is so dedicated, she's continued working there even more then a hundred years after she died!

Mary Elizabeth Elliot bequeathed the money needed to start Elliot hospital in 1880, in honor of her husband, Dr. John Seaver Elliot. It took eight years, but in 1888, the hospital—the first general hospital in all of New Hampshire—was complete. It held a total of twenty-five beds. Many people mistakenly believe that the good natured, matronly ghost who walks the hallways of Elliot Hospital today must be Mary Elizabeth Elliot, staying on to oversee the hospital that was built in her and her husband's names.

However, the Elliot hospital ghost is not that of anyone in the Elliot family; and, despite her calm nature, the ghost had a much more violent beginning then might be expected.

Just a few years after opening, on May 14, 1890, a fire swept through the wing of Elliot Hospital that housed the kitchens, killing one female kitchen worker who was only reported in the newspapers at that time as Mrs. Daniel Harriman. While we may not know Mrs. Harriman's first name, we do know that she must have been an exceptionally caring person. Soon after that wing of the hospital was rebuilt, patients would report smelling cookies and other goodies while traveling the hallways, many talking about how homey and comforting the smell was. What could make possibly be more relaxing then the scent of freshly-baked cookies?

One woman told me that, as a nursing student at the hospital, she came to rely on the ghost to help calm down frightened patients. She said that after spending a lot of time at the building, she started to get a sense for when Mrs. Harriman was around—or not. Patients would instantly become visibly more relaxed at these times, even if they couldn't explain exactly why.

Right:
The Elliot family gravestone marker, in haunted Valley Street Cemetery; the inscription reads, "Founders of Elliot Hospital."

MARY E. ELLIOT,
The founder of the
"ELLIOT HOSPITAL"
BORN
May 22, 1823.
DIED
Mar. 20, 1880.

ELLIOT

There have been many changes to Elliot Hospital since her day, but Mrs. Harriman doesn't seem to notice the changes, or that more then a hundred years have passed. Her spirit sticks to the older parts of the hospital, and reports of her baking disappear altogether during times of construction at the healthcare center. As soon as things quiet down again, or at least quiet down as much as a hospital ever does, people begin to report smelling baked goods all over again. Overall, the spirit of Mrs. Harriman is a welcome addition to the hospital staff. The people who have come in contact with her use words like *comforting* and *reassuring* to describe the spirit whose bedside manner has lasted through the ages.

Right:
The flagpole outside of Elliot Hospital;
the monument underneath is dated
1888, the year the center opened.

Saint Josephs
Middle School

Mike was high up on a ladder, changing light bulbs by himself in the empty gym at Saint Josephs Middle School, when he heard a voice quite distinctly in his right ear, warning him to be careful and watch that he didn't fall. Whenever the brawny maintenance man tells about his brief encounter with the uncanny, he always ends the tale by giving a little lopsided grin, and adding, "If talking to a ghost wasn't going to scare me enough to fall off that ladder, nothing was!"

Mike is convinced that the voice showing such concern for his safety that day was none other then the infamous ghost of Saint Josephs Middle School, Sister Mary.

Long before it became a middle school for boys and girls in Manchester, Saint Josephs was used exclusively as a boys' high school, catering to the Catholic families in the area. It was during this time, or so the stories go, that Sister Mary worked for the school. While chaperoning one of the school dances, Sister Mary fell, or possibly jumped, from a second story balcony and broke her neck. She was pronounced dead on the scene.

The cross atop Saint Josephs Regional Middle School.

But the ghost of Sister Mary is still said to be alive and well, and even now walking the hallways of the school. A few people say they have actually seen her white-robed figure, clutching her rosary to her chest, walking the halls before turning into mist or passing through a wall. Most often, she is heard in the schools gym, warning people to be careful and watching over the students.

The ghost of Sister Mary is seen reflected in mirrors, but if you turn to look to see who is producing the image, there is nothing there that can be seen with the naked eye. The ghost's attraction to the mirror has caused more then one Saint Joseph student to treat the apparition like that of slumber party favorite *Bloody Mary*, but Sister Mary isn't nearly so accommodating as that ghost of legend. If you stand in front of a mirror and chant her name, most likely, the only thing you'll end up seeing, is yourself.

The gym at Saint Josephs goes through light bulbs at an alarming rate. They need replacing constantly. Is this merely one of the problems of old wiring in an old building, or is it another sign of Sister Mary's ghostly presence?

This Manchester middle school is haunted by Sister Mary, a nun who fell to her death at the building.

The Murder of Jonas L. Parker

Jonas L. Parker, a former resident of Lowell, Massachusetts, came to Manchester with his brother in the early 1800s to try to make their fortune in the booming manufacturing town. The more conservative townspeople considered him to be something of a scoundrel, and he only reinforced this opinion when he decided to profit off the baser side of life. Parker opened a saloon and bowling alley, and both establishments quickly became among the most popular in town.

Parker prospered in other ways as well. Although the general opinion of him was negative and he was known to be a paranoid and all around disagreeable fellow, he somehow got himself elected as tax collector for the city! The surprising news of his fledgling political career started many tongues wagging. Parker was known to be a shrewd businessman, but it seemed impossible that a saloon owner would have so much influence in the city government. People soon began to speculate that he had somehow blackmailed the upper-class patrons of his saloon in order to get the position.

Parker and his family lived above the saloon, but he spent his days and nights sitting at his own bar drinking, playing cards, and looking for any opportunity possible to flash his large money wad around.

Parker carried on his person a large wallet that contained not only the proceeds from the bar and bowling alley, but also large amounts of the city's money as well. Since a major part of his job as city tax collector involved receiving large sums of currency, receipting, and making change for the tax-paying citizens of Manchester, Parker had ample occasion to pull out the oversized money bag to show off his good fortune. More then one person questioned the safety, and integrity, of this practice. Parker, it seemed to many people, was just looking for trouble.

Trouble found Parker late in the evening of March 26, 1845, when the hired bartender bellowed that someone was at the door asking to see him. Witnesses, some of whom would later mysteriously retract their statements, said it was a man who told Parker that he had to come as a representative of a mysterious woman who needed to speak to him urgently. Patrons who were on scene to observe the unexpected guest said that Parker didn't ask questions, and seemed to know what the man was talking about. The two conferred together by the door for a few minutes, huddled together against the chilly night air like thieves. After a few minutes, Parker announced he was leaving, hit the key that popped open the saloon register, and stuffed a pile of bills from the cash register into his wallet. Everyone in the place saw him leave with the man. It was the last anyone would see of Jonas L. Parker—alive.

The next morning, his body was discovered several blocks away, in the very outskirts of the city near the woods. Parker's watch and a small wallet containing $1,635 (appearing to be the town's money) were found still inside Parker's pockets. But the larger wallet where he kept the proceeds from the saloon and bowling alley were missing, and there was no way at all to guess how much money he'd taken from the till that night, although everyone agreed the saloon had been packed and it looked like a goodly sum. It was unlikely that anyone familiar with Parker wouldn't have known that he carried two wallets, and it remained a mystery as to why the one had been left behind.

While the motivation behind the brutal murder seemed clear to everyone, the news was still shocking. Parker, who was in his early forties, was considered to be very powerfully built. He had manhandled more then one rowdy drunk from his saloon since opening up shop. It seemed impossible that anyone could have overpowered the contentious man who was so accustomed to fighting. It was obvious from the condition of the crime scene that Parker had not been taken by surprise, nor struck down quickly. All around the body, in the trampled remnants of winter snow and soggy melting ice, were the signs of a desperate struggle. Parker had fought heroically for his life. Next to the body, police discovered Parker's lantern crushed so badly that they could barely tell what it was. He had used it, to no avail, in self defense. Jonas Parker had been beaten severely before his throat was finally cut. A knife and razor was found next to the body, presumably, the ones that had taken his life.

Even if it wasn't entirely unexpected, the murder of Jonas L. Parker was very shocking to the residents of Manchester. There had been very few killings in the city up to this point, and people took it as a sign that things were taking a turn for the worse in their beautiful town. Jonas Parker may not have been entirely well thought of in his life, but he was still considered one of them, and they demanded there be a swift conclusion to the case. The thought of blood-thirsty killers walking around free caused a panic that could not be calmed down until justice was done!

Ultimately, after several years, a group of four men were held and tried for the murder of Jonas L. Parker. But the State's case against them was poor, and, in spite of the bold way the killer had walked into the bar that night, there were no eye witnesses that could undoubtedly place any of the four men at the scene of the crime. The State of New Hampshire suffered a crushing defeat in court, and all four of the accused men walked free. No one was ever found guilty or punished for the murder of Jonas Parker.

As time passed, and no new suspects were caught, people slowly forgot about the murder. Over time, the woods where he had been killed were no longer at the outskirts of Manchester. As the city flourished and grew, the boundary line crept closer and closer to the woods where Parker had lost his life that snowy evening.

Nearly fifty years after the murder took place, Doctor Hiram Hill bought a portion of these woods and had them cleared to build a house. The building of the house went by smoothly and unremarkably. The problems didn't start until the construction crew moved on to constructing other buildings on the property. As soon they began to clear the woods to make room for a proposed carriage house and stable, the problems began in earnest. The construction workers began to complain that every time they put something down, it would disappear. Sometimes, the tools would be found at a later date, far away from where they were originally lost; but more often then not, once something disappeared, it was gone for good. Then the talk of strange noises and odd pockets of freezing, cold air started between the men. The construction crew lost workers left and right, and as talk of the curious happenings spread, it began to get harder and harder to replace the workers that left. No one, it seemed, wanted to be stuck on the crew building Dr. Hill's new house.

When the much reduced crew started laying the foundations for the carriage house, they found a pile of stones that the police had used as a cairn to mark the location of Parker's body, found after the murder. The strange disturbances seemed to get worse, and the workers even began to complain that they would find the change missing from their pockets when they went home for the night. As the tension began to run higher, fights broke out among them, with one man accusing another of being the thief.

The workers were ordered to tear down the cairn that had marked the scene of the grisly murder, and several of the stones were used in the building of the stable. Since then, Dr. Hills house on Manchester Street has never been quite right. Many people hear muffled arguments outside, but when they go to see who's fighting, there is no one there and the noises stop. People seem to fall almost ill, with no cause they can think of. The nausea and headaches stop when they leave the property. People seem to subconsciously avoid walking near the spot where the murder took place, even if they have no idea of the home's bloody history.

While no one has ever actually seen the ghost that haunts this property, there seems to be little doubt that the ghost of Jonas Parker is to blame for the disturbances. Even if you cannot see him, he continues to be difficult—even beyond the grave. People say that if you toss a few coins near the spot where he died, it seems to appease him for a short while and the occurrences die down—for a time.

Stories of Parker's love of money survive so strongly, even to this day, that some people like to joke that he's not mad because his murderers were never punished for their crime against him—he just wants back the money they took from him!

The R. G. Sullivan Building

Chris's sister, Jess, had a few simple requests of him while she was on vacation. If he could watch her cat for the week, drop her car off to be fixed, and then pick her up from work the day she got back, it would be a huge help. Getting the car fixed was no problem, but Chris hated his sister's cat. It was about a hundred years old, and was the fattest, laziest animal the man could even imagine. He liked to tell people that he thought you would have to light the thing on fire just to get it to wake up from its nap half the time. Chris figured the animal was on its last legs, and dreaded the thought of it finally dying while he was responsible for it.

But, all in all, it was an easy-enough animal to take care of, the car was fixed promptly, and Chris hardly even realized a whole week had passed, when his sister gave him a call from work announcing the taxi had just brought her from the airport, and would he mind coming to get her at eight instead of five? After a week away, she had a lot of catching up to do.

Chris always admired the building where his sister worked. Formerly, it was a cigar factory that produced R. G. Sullivan's world famous 7-20-4 cigars. During the high point of the brand's popularity, the cigar factory on Canal Street rolled out fifty-four million cigars a year. Chris sometimes saw old ashtrays and cigar boxes marked with the distinctive R. G. Sullivan 7-20-4 logo up for auction on eBay, and they seemed to be popular with collectors.

Of course, there had been some big changes for the R. G Sullivan building since the cigar company had closed. The seven-floor building was now home to upscale office suites, having been completely renovated in 1986 by Brady Sullivan Properties, and it was such a success that many developers took notice of the project. Shortly after the R. G. Sullivan building was reborn, a bunch of the old mills and factories along the Merrimack started getting snapped up and done over.

Eight o'clock came and went, and Chris's cell phone was silent. He knew full well his sister was up in her nice air-conditioned office, while he was trapped in her steamy car, with her mangy cat, down in the parking lot. Finally getting fed up with waiting, he snatched up the cat carrier and walked into the building. It looked like it was pretty empty; it seemed like his sister was planning on being the last one out. Vacation or no, Chris knew his sister was a terrible workaholic. She'd probably stay up there, typing away, all night if no one was there to make her go home.

When Jess saw her brother walk in, lugging the cat carrier behind him, she suddenly realized how late she had stayed in the building. It was unusual for her to stay so late. More often then not, if she had work to do, she took it home with her for the night. Workers in other offices in the building had told her that when the R. G. Sullivan Building was still a cigar factory, a lot of kids had worked there and been injured. There were plenty of ghost stories told about these child laborers around the water cooler. People even said that from the outside of the building, you could see kids standing at the windows, waving frantically, like they were trying to get you to notice they were trapped inside. She knew that tenants on other floors had complained about strange noises that no one ever found the cause of. People blamed the ghosts for all kinds of things that went wrong in the building. If the water in the drinking fountain tasted a little metallic to them, they said it was caused by the ghosts. If someone misplaced an important document, the ghosts had taken it. No one liked staying any later then they had to at the building.

Jess didn't think that she really believed in the stories about the ghosts, but even *she* had to admit that the thought of dead children creeped her out when she was stuck there alone at night.

Jess was in a hurry to get home after being away for so long, but as soon as she saw her cat she couldn't help herself. Cooing to the old fluff ball like he was a long-lost child, she opened up the door to his cage and let him out into the office. Her bosses would never know . . . hopefully. The cat *did* seem to shed a lot more in its old age then it use to.

The old cat was fine—until he was lifted from the cage. Like a streak of lightning he flung himself around the room, spitting and clawing at furniture. Chris tried to grab the cat, but all he got for his trouble was a pair of stinging scratches down his arm.

Former site of the famous R. G. Sullivan 7-20-04 Cigar Factory;
today the space is used for offices.

With an ear splitting yowl, the cat suddenly froze. Looking directly at an empty spot in front of it, the cat arched its back, flattened its ears, and started to hiss viciously. The feline even grew brave enough to take a few swipes, with its claws extended, at whatever it thought was there.

Together, Chris and Jess were able to manhandle the hissing, clawing animal back into the plastic pet carrier. As much as he disliked cats, even Chris felt bad for the poor thing. Its bravado was all show. Once he got his hands on the feline, he could feel the way it was shaking in fear. Chris told her sister to get her stuff together, *right now*, and they were getting out of there. He couldn't imagine the lazy geriatric cat reacting that way just because of the spirits of kids. One thing for sure, his sister wouldn't be staying late at work by herself, ever again.

The Grandmotherly Ghost

Sarah knew how lucky she and her family were to have such a nice apartment in such a safe quiet neighborhood. She, her husband, and their little girl lived upstairs from the old woman who owned the building, and Josie was everything anyone could ever hope for in a landlord. Josie, who had no family of her own, adored Sarah's three-year-old daughter. It was not long after they moved in that the little girl started to call the kindly old woman Grandma Josie. Sarah's own mother had passed away long before her daughter was born, and she was thrilled that the little girl finally had a Grandma figure in her life.

Grandma Josie was a spirited, soft-hearted woman who loved having the young family live upstairs. When she knew that Sarah and her husband Bill would be working late, she would bake them a casserole so they wouldn't have to worry about supper that night. Some nights their daughter stayed overnight in her apartment so Sarah and Bill could have a night to themselves. All in all, the upstairs tenants became like the family that Josie never had.

A series of small strokes struck Josie very suddenly, and they all knew that, for awhile at least, she wouldn't be able to live on her own anymore. Sarah and Bill both worked full time, and as much as they would have loved to take the time off to take care of the woman who had been so kind to them, there was no way it would be possible. While Josie underwent physical therapy to try to regain her skills, she would have to be moved into a nursing home, but they all assured each other that the move was only temporary, and she'd be back in her apartment in no time.

Several weeks later, Sarah was awakened by the sound of slamming doors downstairs, and the angry buzz of the fire alarms. She sniffed cautiously but couldn't smell any smoke. Fearing that teenagers had learned the apartment was empty and were causing grief in Josie's home, she called the fire and police departments and rushed her family out the door.

The fire department found no evidence of a break in or a fire—they were at a loss to explain why the alarms had gone off. Stranger still, they said, all the clocks in the house had stopped at 3:16 a.m., the time when the noise had first woken Sarah up.

Early the next morning, the nursing home called Sarah. Josie had suffered another stroke during the night, and this time it was fatal. In a shaky voice, already starting to cry, Sarah asked what time Josie had passed on. They told her that time of death was given as 3:16 a.m.

No one was more surprised then Sarah when they found out that Josie had left the duplex to them. They continued to live on in the house, and eventually rented out the downstairs to a young couple that reminded them of themselves when Josie had given them their break.

Both Sarah's daughter and the little girl who moved downstairs would tell their mothers about their nice Grandma, who visited them at night. Sarah passed it off as little girls' fantasy, or maybe a story the girls were having between themselves, until she too began to sense the presence in the house. There was never anything scary about the unseen presence. Sometimes, Sarah would catch the scent of an old-fashioned lavender sachet as she walked through the building. During times of stress, the smell would become more noticeable, and Sarah described feeling enveloped by the smell and how it gave her a warm protected feeling. It was like being hugged, ever so gently, by a warm summer cloud.

After awhile, everyone in the house got use to Josie being around, and they would strike up conversations with her when they felt as though her spirit was around. If Sarah couldn't remember where she had put something down, she'd ask Josie, and more often then not when Sarah turned around, she'd find the item on the table behind her, in plain sight.

The clocks, in both apartments, tended to stop suddenly at 3:16, but other then that, the grandmotherly ghost of Josie was a welcome addition to both families. As the two little girls got older, the presence of the woman started to fade away, and was felt less and less. By the time they were old enough to move out on their own, Josie's ghost had continued on its journey, apparently feeling the girls didn't need quite so much protection anymore.

A Not So Helpful Spirit

It is interesting to note that the house where this ghostly roommate took up residence is located on River Road. Two more hauntings that are talked about later in this book are also associated with this quiet residential neighborhood in Manchester—the River Road Jogger and the haunting at one of the abandoned buildings at the Youth Detention Center. Something about the beautiful homes or the friendly atmosphere of the area must make spirits feel at home.

Using money she had recently won in her divorce settlement from her ex-husband, Marie was able to buy her dream home on River Road. The place was huge, ridiculously so, considering she was just one person on her own; but she loved the house, loved the neighborhood, and loved how friendly all the people around her were. It was the kind of neighborhood where people got together and sipped ice tea while their kids rode bikes or played basketball in the driveway. Most of the houses had stunning gardens, and Maria couldn't wait for the chilly spring to turn into summer so she could find out how green her thumb was.

But the cold, wet spring lingered on, and the house on River Road always seemed to have a perpetual chill in its air. Maria kept the heat going non-stop, but whenever she left, she was always very careful to turn the heat back down to a reasonable temperature. It was better for the environment, and for her wallet, too. Ironically, soon Maria would be dreaming of the days when her only problem was that the house was always too cold.

Within a few weeks of moving in, without fail, and no matter how sure she was that she had turned off the heat when she left, Maria always came home to a sauna. Upon checking the thermostat, it would show that it had been cranked up as high as it would go—much higher then she ever put it on, to be sure. After a few weeks, it started to happen even when she was home. She'd set the heat at sixty-eight degrees, go make herself some tea in the kitchen, and by the time she walked back into the living room, the thermometer would read ninety. Servicemen were called to the house, but they couldn't find a thing wrong with her heating system or her temperature gauge. The diminutive blonde got into the habit of leaving her windows open with fans set in them, no matter what the temperature outside, and always wore a tank top under her clothes, since she couldn't seem to control the heat in her own house. She'd go out for the day in comfy sweaters that she would have to peel off immediately as soon as she walked through the door.

Then the silly games started with her windows, too. Maria would turn off the heat and shut and lock the windows, only to find the heat on high and the windows wide open when she came home—even when she was just gone for a quick minute, running errands or borrowing something from a neighbor. Feeling foolish, Maria asked the young couple that lived next door to her to let her know if they ever saw anyone hanging around the house, and they promised to keep an eye on her place whenever she left. Between the three of them, Maria was sure, they would catch whoever was opening and shutting her windows.

Then the curious happenings began to focus on Maria's possessions. The houseplants she struggled to keep alive would be tipped over in their pots, and the dirt scattered all over the floor if she turned her back on them for a second. Red clothes would mysteriously find their way into the washing machine when she was doing a load of whites, no matter how carefully Maria sorted the clothes before putting them in. She'd wake up in the middle of the night when the lights flicked on, and they'd turn themselves off—but only after she had gotten up out of bed and pulled her slippers on. Other times it was the radio in the kitchen that went on during the early hours of the morning, turned to a station that played only static with the volume on full blast.

Even more annoying was the way that trouble always seemed to start just when Maria was beginning to relax. When all she wanted to do was soak in a nice warm bubble bath for awhile, loud thumping noises would, without fail, draw her up out of the tub just as soon as she had climbed in to relax. If she curled up on the sofa to read a book, and left her cozy spot to go into the kitchen for something to drink, when she came back, her page would be lost. Or the book would be missing altogether!

Maria was, by nature, a neat and tidy person. *A place for everything, and everything in its place*, was her motto. But even though she put her things away religiously, she always had to watch her step in the house on River Road. If she turned around suddenly, or got up at night to use the bathroom, more likely then not, she'd end up flat on her face, tripped by some obstacle that had been placed on the floor.

The final straw came one morning when Maria stepped outside to check to see if her newspaper had been delivered, just to have the front door slam shut in her face and lock. Trapped outside, with no shoes and in just her pajamas and a short robe, Maria lost it and started banging on the door. Her neighbor heard the noise and came over to see what was going on. When the neighbor tried the door, the knob turned easily in her hands and admitted the two women inside, as if it had never been locked.

Maria was completely mortified, convinced that her neighbor must think she had been lying about the door being locked. When she realized that the neighbor didn't think any such thing, the whole story came pouring out of her—the heat, and the lights, and the night-time crashes to the floor tripped up by shoes she knew she had left downstairs in the kitchen. It felt wonderful to finally let it all out and to have someone listen with a sympathetic ear. Maria didn't care if her neighbor ended up thinking she was crazy; she was just tried of keeping it all bottled up inside of her.

The neighbor asked Maria if she had tried talking to the spirit that was tormenting her. As funny as it is to say, this was actually the first moment that it really dawned on Maria that she was being haunted. She had always believed in ghosts, but never expected to ever live with one herself. Feeling more then a little silly, she followed her neighbor's lead and walked from room to room asking the entity to please leave, or to at least leave her alone. She told the entity that she would do her best to not bother it, if it would do the best it could not to bother her. Maria may have felt dumb while she was doing it, but it actually worked. All the ghostly activity stopped as of that day and never returned to the house on River Road. Maria lived in the house for many years and none of the problems she had when she first moved in were repeated. When, eventually, she moved to a different city, she kept in touch with the new owners of the house, curious to see if the ghost that had bothered her for so long, would start back up again. But if anything strange was going on in the house on River Road, they never mentioned it to Maria.

Avery

9 15 Elm Street used to be a restaurant called the Psaris Bistro. After that, it was bought by a former Manchester mayor (who had once run for Governor of New Hampshire), Bob Shaw. He quickly turned it into a popular place for the local lunch crowd, dubbing his place, Bob Shaw's Italian Sub Shop. But no matter what name the small Elm Street restaurant goes under, it comes complete with its very own ghost.

While he probably already knew about the ghost, Bob Shaw, who was use to media attention himself, was probably a little surprised that Avery drew so much more attention then *he* did. The ghost that haunts the shop is nearly as much of a Manchester landmark as Bob Shaw himself. Avery, as the Psaris Bistro owners dubbed the friendly spirit, makes sure his presence is known. Luckily there's nothing frightening about Avery, so he doesn't scare off the customers.

Most of Avery's repertoire includes classic poltergeist phenomena, and some people have mistaken him for one. Poltergeists, which is roughly translated from German for *noisy ghosts*, have well-known, carefully researched haunting patterns. Poltergeist activity usually consists of loud raps or thumps, knocking noises in walls or on floors, things moving on their own, sometimes violently, and bed-shaking episodes. Poltergeists are almost never seen, and, rarely, do they speak. Poltergeists seem to start up pretty quickly, make things downright unlivable for awhile, and then, as time goes on, the phenomena peters out slowly, until it stops completely. The average duration of a poltergeist event is several months, although there have been reputable recorded cases that lingered for years, or others that passed in just hours. This type of haunting normally centers around just one person, usually that of a young girl or boy just entering puberty.

Prevailing wisdom is that a poltergeist is not a ghost or spirit at all. Instead, the occurrences are thought to be subconscious, uncontrollable psychokinetic talents caused by the person whom the haunting is centering around. The thought is that with the in rush of hormones as puberty approaches, wild talents, like telekinesis, are unlocked in the child's brain, even though they themselves aren't aware that they have such gifts.

The ghost at Bob Shaw's Italian Sub Shop does share some of these characteristics—he has never been seen, aside from a few shadows flitting across a mirror, if he thinks he is being ignored, utensils tend to move through the air, and rapping noises are heard on the floors and walls of the tiny Elm Street eatery. There seems to be a certain mischievousness to a lot of poltergeist pranks, and this too is an attitude that Avery shares with so called noisy ghosts.

However, Avery differs from the classic pattern of poltergeist activity as much as he matches them.

A friendly ghost named Avery has taken up residence
at Bob Shaw's Italian Sub Shop on Elm Street.

The occurrences at Bob Shaw's Italian Sub Shop have been well known and reported for years.

It seems as though Avery has always been there; he didn't just suddenly start banging pots one day out of the blue, and it doesn't look like he's going anywhere else anytime soon. There is also no center or focus person who brings Avery out. Many people have experienced the ghost, most of them more then once.

Avery is also unlike a poltergeist in his vocal abilities. So far, there are only two known cases of poltergeists speaking. Avery has the reputation for being a chatter box. The most commonly heard complaints about the loquacious ghost is that he just won't shut up! Many people have heard Avery speak. Names being called by no one, and lighthearted conversation just a smidge too low to make out the words, are typical at Bob Shaw's Sub Shop. Once Avery's presence is acknowledged, usually the chattering ends and you can get back to your meal.

Whether a ghost or poltergeist, or something in between, one thing is for sure: Avery is here to stay, and he likes a little attention every now and then. His antics only seem to get worse the longer that he is ignored. Regular customers make it a point to say *hi* if they feel like there is a presence nearby, if only because they don't want their lunch interrupted by missing salt shakers, or forks that won't sit still. Avery has generated a lot of media attention over the years; he's a regular feature when Halloween time comes around, and knowing how Avery is, he probably loves all the attention.

The Horror
on Hanover Street

This story was told to me second or third hand (or possibly, more like fourth or fifth). It is so outrageously scary that it's hard to imagine that it could be real . . . or perhaps the problem is that it is just so frightening, it makes you not want to believe it *could* be real! Is the following a tale of a truly terrible ghost that tormented a young woman and her two-year-old son, or the product of the distortions that come up after a few retellings? You'll have to decide that for yourself.

Leslie was in a tough spot. She had a young son she was trying to raise all on her own, with very little money, and needed to find someplace to live that was close enough to her job that she could walk or take the bus to work. She called real estate offices and searched the internet and want ads, desperately trying to find an apartment she could afford that was in the location she was looking for. Things didn't look promising for the single mother. Her lease on her current apartment was coming up for renewal in just a few days, and the landlord had already warned her that if she chose to stay on, he would have to raise her rent by $200 a month. There was no way around it—Leslie had to find a new place to live. And fast.

Walking up Hanover Street one day on her lunch break, mulling over what to do, she noticed a *For Rent* sign in the window of one of the buildings. Instantly, Leslie whipped out her cell phone and punched in the number on the sign. When the landlord told her what the rent was for the two bedroom apartment, she nearly dropped her phone. It was almost half of what her current rent was for a one bedroom in a much worse neighborhood. The landlord assured her that there was nothing wrong with the apartment. The other tenants in the building were quiet and friendly. The apartment had just been repainted, and he'd bought all new appliances for the unit. The one catch was that he was going to be out of town for a few weeks and couldn't show her the apartment until he got back. Leslie hesitated for just a single moment, then impulsively told the landlord she didn't have a few weeks and she'd take the apartment sight unseen as long as she could start moving in immediately. The landlord was surprised but happy to have someone who could move in so soon. They made arrangements for her to pick up her keys from a downstairs neighbor, and she would sign a lease when the landlord got back from his vacation.

Happy with her newfound luck, Leslie went home to start getting things together in time for the big move. She did her best to ignore that niggling feeling in the back of her head that kept trying to remind her of what a bad idea it was to agree to live in a place she'd never even seen before. Leslie reminded the voice that she didn't really have a lot of options. It would be fine; it was better then a cardboard box, and no place could be that bad, especially on such a nice street.

The next day, showing up at her new home with a cranky two-year-old and a pile of belongings that little *Nervous Nellie* voice cried out triumphantly. *I told you so*, a little voice seemed to tell her from the back of mind. It was right. Leslie couldn't quite put her finger on it, but there was something just not quite right about the new apartment. Oh, it was everything the landlord had promised it would be—a well-maintained, freshly-painted, large two bedroom with a multitude of windows to let in the sunlight. Honestly, it was the nicest place Leslie had ever lived in. But for whatever reason, the old, cramped one bedroom for twice as much money began to sound really good to Leslie. If only she hadn't already told her original landlord she'd be leaving!

The first few weeks in the new apartment went by, and while Leslie couldn't shake her bad feelings about the place, she also couldn't have said what it was, specifically, that she didn't like about the new place.

It really is such a cute apartment, she'd tell herself, *and look at how much money we're saving by being here.*

But at night sometimes, when she came home from work, she felt as though someone was watching her. Not someone on the street, or another tenant in the building, but someone right there in her apartment. Sometimes, when she walked into a room, she would get the sense that she wasn't alone, even though there was no one else to be found. Leslie didn't know how to describe the feeling, she just knew that she always felt a presence nearby.

One night, she decided to treat her son to a little movie, and she let him stay up late to watch the latest Disney cartoon on DVD with her. Again, she had that eerie feeling that she was being watched. When she looked up at the hallway leading out of the living room, she saw the shadow of a tall man, with a slight build. It looked as though he was standing in the moonlight at the window at the end of the hallway!

Leslie jumped up, grabbed the phone, and ran into the hallway to see who was there. The hallway was empty! She tried in vain to come up with a reasonable explanation for what could have caused the shadow, but she knew what she had seen. It had been unmistakably that of a very thin man.

After that night, it was as though all Hell had broken loose in the Hanover Street apartment. Not one day would go by without something being hurtled across the room and smashed. The sound of a man's heavy footsteps walking back and forth, up and down, the hallway each night would keep Leslie awake until dawn, when she'd finally be so exhausted the noise couldn't keep her awake any longer and she would slip into a fitful sleep. She had terrible nightmares every night she slept in that apartment—from the first day she moved in. She woke up still tired, snapping at everything her son did, and with little motivation to go to work or see her friends. *If only I could just get one full night of rest,* she would think.

Sometimes, a stench of decay would flood the apartment—it would come on so strongly and suddenly that Leslie would gag and throw up. She got frustrated when she couldn't find the source of the smell and called an exterminator in to see if he thought maybe a mouse—well okay a **LOT** of mice—could have gotten stuck in the walls and died there. She knew it was a stretch, but Leslie was looking desperately for a rational explanation for the stink that sometimes filled the apartment. And, of course, the disgusting smell didn't start up while the exterminator was there, and he never found any evidence that Leslie had mice at all. She called two more exterminators to the apartment, hoping to get a different opinion, but they all said the same thing. Leslie couldn't reproduce the smell when anyone was there, and she started to catch people giving her odd looks when she talked about it. Leslie wished that, just once, someone other then her would smell that terrible smell, if only just so she would know her mind wasn't playing tricks on her! The only person she had to verify that there was indeed an awful reek in the apartment was her two-year-old son, who most people did not exactly consider to be the most reliable witness.

Finally, one night the ghost seemed to take a break and the apartment was free of pounding footsteps for once. Leslie gave a sigh of relief. Maybe whatever terrible thing was afflicting the apartment was over. At the very least, perhaps she could finally get a good nights sleep. Unfortunately, Leslie's prayers were not answered. She was awoken late that night, not by foot steps, but by the sound of her young son screaming in terror in his bedroom.

She flung back the covers and hopped out of bed in a flash, tearing down the hallway to her son's room. It was as cold as ice in the room, even though it was a hot July night, and Leslie didn't own an air conditioner. She found her son huddled under his covers, cowering away from the closet door.

"The bad man!" the young boy wailed. "The bad, bad, man!!"

When Leslie sat on the bed to comfort him, it almost felt as though the bed was shaking, but she couldn't tell if it was bed or just her. No matter how much she tried to convince the little boy it was just a bad dream, he insisted there was something scary living in his closet.

After that, the haunting got worse. And violent. Often times, out of no where, Leslie would feel hands slap her, pinch her arms, and twice she even felt strong blows to her face. She could do nothing to protect herself, and that seemed to make the ghost grow bolder. One night, she woke up to a freezing cold room and couldn't move her body at all. It even felt like there was a huge weight on her chest that was keeping her from filling her lungs with air. Leslie started to panic, afraid that she was about to pass out, and maybe even be slowly suffocated. The petrified young woman pulled together all the strength she had, and with a silent prayer to God, used all her might just to sit up. Somehow she did it. As soon as she was sitting up, she could breathe normally again, and as she did, she heard a man's voice scream so loud, her windows rattled and shook. The smell of rot and death was suddenly overpowering, stronger now then it ever had been before in the apartment.

Is one of the apartments on Hanover Street
hiding something terrifying?

That was that, as far as Leslie was concerned. She didn't know what to do, other then to snatch up her son and leave. She spent the rest of the night just driving around aimlessly, picking streets at random, and trying to figure out what she was going to do, while her son slept in the backseat of the car.

Finally, Leslie turned to her mother for advice. She had been so scared of not being believed that, other then her complaints about the bad smell, she had told no one about the strange events going on in the Hanover Street apartment. Leslie's mother got very worried when she heard the horrifying tale, but she wasn't concerned about any possibility of there being a ghost in the apartment; she thought Leslie was probably severely overworked and overtired. Her daughter looked terrible; she had lost at least fifteen pounds in the past month, and there were dark circles under her eyes. Not to mention the awful bruises on her arms! Leslie's mother wondered briefly if her daughter had gotten involved with a man who was violent with her. Maybe she had even taken up drugs! Where else would she have come up with these wild tales? Leslie's mother told her to go out and relax for the evening with her friends and she would babysit at the apartment that night. It would all look better if she would just get out and have some fun for once.

Leslie did go out with some friends and started to feel so much better, she began to think that her mother must have been right. She was tired all the time, and she had been working hard; there was so much pressure on her as the sole parent in the household.

The things she thought were happening at home couldn't be real. Could they? Out that night with her friends, all the bad experiences of the past few weeks started to take on the hazy unreality of a bad dream.

Refreshed and renewed, Leslie came home to chaos. The first thing she saw as she pulled up in front of the building, was that her mother was sitting on the front steps of the apartment building holding her sleeping son, who was wrapped in a blanket. The woman was pale and shaking, demanding that Leslie pack her things, that instant, and leave the apartment immediately. Not next week, not tomorrow morning, not when she found a new place to live, but that very night. They could come stay with her if they had no place else to go; it didn't matter, just as long as they didn't try to stay in the apartment. As Leslie bundled the two into her car and began the drive to her mother's, the woman told her what had happened this eventful evening—but first she apologized for ever doubting that there was a malicious ghost in the Hanover Street apartment.

Her evening had seemed normal enough at first. She and her grandson had played a few rounds of *Go Fish* and had a great time, even though, every so often, she would catch a whiff of something rotten wafting through the room. At eight, she gave her grandson a bath and put him to bed. Tired after a few hours of trying to keep up with a rambunctious two-year-old, she sat down at the kitchen table and laid out a hand of *Solitaire*. There was a sudden feeling that someone had walked into the room with her. She turned around in her chair, expecting to see that her grandson had gotten up and needed something. Instead, she was met with a blast of wintry air. Just as quickly, the cold air seemed to melt away, and she, perplexed but not yet frightened, turned back to her game. Squealing against the kitchen linoleum, the chair next to hers at the table was pulled back, as if someone she couldn't see just sat down. Then her cards began to get tossed around, all moved by a pair of unseen hands. Frightened, she shouted for whomever was doing it to stop. It did, but the deathly stench persisted, and she couldn't stand being in the apartment one more minute. Even with nothing happening, it was obvious that some type of malignant presence was still there in the room with her.

Deciding that she needed a cup of tea to help calm her nerves, Leslie's mother turned on the kitchen faucet to fill the kettle for tea. An aroma of the grave filled the small kitchen, and the water came out muddy and thick. That was the last straw. She packed up her grandson and left. She could have sworn that she heard laughter behind her as she locked the door.

The next day, Leslie left, too. She wrote the landlord a terse note, left her keys with the neighbor downstairs, and thanked her lucky stars she had never signed an official lease for the haunted apartment on Hanover Street. Now she knew why the landlord was willing to rent out such prime real estate for so cheap a price.

Hesser College

On Jen's first day at Hesser College, the other girls who lived on her floor gave her two pieces of advice. The first was to never leave any of her clothes unattended in the second-floor laundry room. The second was to shower only during the day—never, never, never at night in the girls' bathroom. It wasn't long before she found out the wisdom in those warnings.

The first piece of advise she disregarded was about the second floor laundry. If someone really wanted to steal her socks that badly, they could have them, she figured. She soon found it wasn't theft she needed to be worried about. The first time Jen left her laundry there, she came back to find all her freshly dried loads sopping wet and back in the washers. She thought perhaps someone had gotten confused and had been trying to be helpful, though she couldn't figure out why someone would take the clothes from the dryer to the washer. But she figured it was an honest mistake and let it go.

The next time she walked back into the sunny second-floor laundry room to find all her clothes, again soaked, dumped in the middle of the floor. As she bent to pick them up and rewash them, she discovered that several other students' clothes had been tossed into the mix. It took awhile, but she and the other girls were able to sort it all out eventually—even though it looked like some of the clothing was now missing for some.

Entrance to the Hesser Center Building, home to Hesser College, office suites, and more then a few ghosts.

Now Jen was steamed. It wasn't like there weren't enough washers to go around! Why do something so stupid to a bunch of people you didn't even know!?

Jen ranted and raved about it for a few days, until finally one of the other girls on her floor took her aside and explained it to her. It wasn't students who were causing mischief in the laundry room. It was ghosts. Now Jen was more convinced then ever that everyone at school must hate her. Did they think she was stupid? A ghost? Did they really expect her to believe such a thing?

The next time Jen took her laundry down to the second floor, it was empty. She loaded the washer, read a book in a chair, positioned so she could keep her eye on her laundry, and when the buzzer sounded, she moved the wet items herself to the large industrial dryers stacked along the wall. She watched them spin mindlessly for a few minutes until her cell phone started to ring. Since she couldn't get reception in the laundry room, she stood just outside the door and took the call from her mother. Just as Jen hung up, the dryer buzzed angrily that it was done. But when she looked, it was empty.

What the heck had happened to all her clothes?!

After lifting the lid on several washing machines, she found them, again, soaking wet, crumpled in a heap at the bottom of the washer. Only this time, Jen knew for sure that no one had entered the laundry room the whole time her clothes had been drying. Even when she took the phone call, no one could have walked past her into the room without her knowing. So who had moved the clothes?

This second floor laundry room is home to a prank-playing spirit.

The mischievous prank-playing (or annoying, prank-playing, I guess you would think if it was *your* clothes getting played with) ghost in the second floor laundry room is only one of many ghosts that haunt the halls and classrooms of the Hesser College building. What few people realize about the center is that the building probably holds the distinction of being the most haunted place in Manchester. It may have taken Jen awhile to learn her lesson as far as the laundry room was concerned, but after listening to the stories she wasn't even going to test the warning she had been given about the girls' bathroom.

The strange occurrences in the girls' bathroom at Hesser College have long been whispered about. Few freshman make it through their first day without someone taking them aside and giving them the traditional warning: "The bathroom is fine—during the day. Don't shower at night, no matter what." While Hesser has more then its share of ghosts and paranormal phenomena, they are all of a pretty innocent nature, and students get use to sharing their space with specters. All except the one in the bathroom, that is. It is the one haunting, and people aren't even sure if it should be classified as a haunting, that no one ever gets use to, no matter how long they live at the school. Terrible, horrifying noises are sometimes heard by people who use the bathroom at night. The unnerving, otherworldly, sounds are usually described as a horrific howling noise. To some people, they sound like a mass of human voices, all screaming in terror at once, other people liken the sound to a large animal growling, but others say that the noise is like nothing they can explain, that it is not of this planet. The noises are a mystery. No one has ever been able to trace what may be causing the howling in the girls' bathroom, either structurally or supernaturally.

While the source of the howling is unknown, the other ghosts at Hesser College have a much more earthly explanation. They seem to be the spirits of children who once worked in the old building when it was a shoe factory. The school, or factory as it was back then, is located right on the banks of the river, and during one of the yearly spring floods that were common in Manchester in the 1800s, the waters were said to have gone as high as the third floor. Several child laborers were trapped during this flood and died. No one has seen the laundry room ghost, but it is generally assumed to be that of one of these children.

The other ghostly children at Hesser aren't nearly as frightening as the strange happenings in the bathroom. The most well known of these ghosts is that of a young boy who can be heard playing and bouncing a rubber ball in the rear stairwell of the building. The sound of his laughter and his small footsteps as he chases after the ball can be heard at any hour of the day or night. When students have tried to lay in wait, hoping to 'catch' the ghost, the noises stop and then immediately start up again somewhere else entirely, as if the whole thing is a really fun game. The little boy seems to like playing hide and seek with the living.

The second ghost in the back stairwell is not quite so playful. No one has seen this apparition, but his heavier footsteps indicate not that of a child, but that of a full-grown man. The footsteps seem to follow after those of a little boy as he plays with his toy.

Two ghosts have made the back stairwells at Hesser their homes. The sign on this door warns students that it is locked and to use the elevator. Such signs are taken as proof of the hauntings by some students.

Some people have guessed that perhaps this spirit was a Forman at the shoe factory, or maybe even the child's father. The little boy seems frightened of this ghost, and once the heavier noise of the man begins, the little boy disappears for awhile. The sounds of his playing won't start up again until the man's presence fades away. More sensitive students have described the man as having a very dark energy, or being a very negative spirit; though when you compare him to the screeching in the girls' bathroom, he suddenly seems a lot less ominous.

The fourth floor of the building, in particular, is practically overrun with ghostly children. They chatter and laugh incessantly, and security logs a lot of complaints about the noise. A former Hesser security guard was in for a fright one night when he went to investigate a complaint on the fourth floor. After getting several angry calls about a bunch of children singing to each other, he headed up on the elevator to take a look. When the doors slid open, he caught sight of a tiny emaciated little girl sitting on the floor by the bathroom. The security guard walked over to her to ask who she was and to see if she was waiting for her mommy to be done in the bathroom. The little girl raised her head, looked him straight in the eyes, and winked out of existence. It wasn't until that moment that the security guard realized that what he had seen was not a little girl, but instead, something not of this world.

The little girl by the bathroom may be the same ghost as the one who is known for writing on windows. Sometimes, in the frost on the oversized windows of the building, students find shaky, poorly-spelled messages begging for help. It is rare, but not unheard of, for students get a glimpse of cold blues eyes, or the reflection of a small girl, in the window as well, when the messages are found. Stories say this little girl died of hypothermia in the mill when a cold snap came in on the tail of one of Manchester's many spring floods, and that she is searching for help even today.

This fourth floor hallway is home to several ghostly children who can be heard laughing and playing at all hours of the night.

Hesser College occupies only part of the building that bears its name. The other half is leased to high-profile firms like Edwards and Kelcy and AT&T. Workers in the offices at the Hesser Center Building have also reported hearing children playing in the hallways. In fact, one man told me that he heard the noises so often, and so loudly, when he was first hired, that he asked his boss to speak to the owner of the daycare to ask her to please keep the noise down so people could get some work done. It was then that this man was icily informed by his boss that there was no daycare in the building, and not to spread the story around. He said they had a hard enough time trying to get people to stay late as it was, with all the ghost stories that were flying about.

This boss isn't the only one who would like to quiet the creepy tales surrounding the school. Officials at Hesser College are notoriously tight lipped about the stories that have been circulating about the facility. Rumors abound that the locked stairwells in the building are actually kept off limits due to the multitude of ghostly activity reported there. They also do not respond to media requests about their ghosts. The largest acknowledgement Hesser has publicly made about the ghost stories was reported in the Hippo newspaper when one official was quoted as dismissing the tales by saying, "It's an old building, there are likely to be sounds."

The Hesser Center Building.

An Apartment Building on Beech Street

The manager of a three-story apartment building on Beech Street couldn't figure out why he couldn't keep tenants in the place. People moved out abruptly, complaining of strange noises and smells, or giving no explanation for their departure at all. He decided that maybe he needed to do a little cleaning up around the place, and asked a neighborhood kid to come help him do a clean sweep of the building, starting in the basement and working their way up. He figured they could clean the place up a little, do some minor repair work, and maybe his tenants would be happier. Then perhaps he wouldn't always have empty apartments that needed renting in the building. The building was at least a hundred years old; it would be a shame to let such a beauty of a structure fall into disrepair like that, anyway.

The basement was eerie looking, filled with cobwebs and broken bits of furniture that he had always meant to throw out, but had somehow, instead, found a way down to the lower levels to be forgotten. With the help of his neighbor's kid, Tommy, they were able to get even the heavy pieces out of there. As they lifted the last piece of trash, an oversized headboard, with a crack down the center, came away from the wall and Tommy noticed a door knob sticking out from behind it.

It had been so long since he'd been down there, even the owner of the building had forgotten that the small room in the basement was there. He remembered that there had been some old boxes stacked inside the little room when he bought the place and figured it was as good a time as any to finally get rid of them.

Tommy grabbed a hold of the knob and gave it a turn—with the way things were going already, those few boxes probably meant a ton of crap covered in spiders and God only knows what else inside. The landlord hadn't warned him it was going to be like this when he'd asked him to come help him out for a day. Tommy knew he was probably going to be stuck there the rest of the day, hauling out a bunch of junk, and listening to the old guy go on and on about how nice the building must have looked back in the day.

As soon as Tommy turned the door knob, it was turned, forcibly, back into position from the other side of the doorway. Tommy struggled with the door a few more times and finally got the knob to work properly, but as soon as he managed to push the door open a few inches, something from behind the door pushed it back, shutting it with a loud bang. When Tommy tried opening it again, the door was locked. The landlord, who had been watching the whole struggle, told Tommy that he had never had a key for the basement room; he'd never even known that it could lock. Scared now, the landlord and the kid ran out of the basement, and the landlord locked the door behind him.

Now the landlord was taking the tenants complaints a little more seriously, and decided he needed to figure out what was going on. After talking to a few tenants, he got the idea that his apartment building was very, very haunted, and he probably needed to get some kind of professional help with his problem.

The crew from Ghost Quest, Manchester's local paranormal research group, came out to the building a few weeks later. Starting in the attic, they were instantly confronted with the spirits of two children, who it appeared, had lived in the building when they were alive. Also in the building was an older woman and her husband. The psychic got the sense that the couple loved the building and perhaps had been former owners of it themselves. The couple gave the sense that they very much wanted to stay on there.

Walking down to the next floor, the investigative team was nearly overpowered by the smell of beer. Even though the manager told them he didn't smell it right then, he did tell them that it wasn't an unusual occurrence to smell alcohol on that floor, even when the apartment was empty and had been sitting there unrented for months at a time. It seems the building has an alcoholic ghost! In the apartment on this floor, people have sometimes reported seeing a figure walk from the living room to the kitchen, presumably going to get another beer. Sometimes, they could even see an impression on furniture in the living room, as if someone invisible were sitting down.

Ghost Quest was able to channel some of the spirits residing in the apartment building and helped several of them move on, though they felt it only fair that the older couple who loved the place so much got to stay on.

The Palace Theatre

The Palace Theatre was built in 1914 to be a smaller version of its New York City namesake. The theatre was a powerhouse of entertainment during the years of Vaudeville comedy. It drew in huge headlining names like Harry Houdini, the Marx Brothers, Jimmy Durante, and even Bob Hope graced its stage.

At the time it opened, advertisement for the Palace boasted that the theatre was the only one in all of Manchester that was both fire proof (Manchester was known for its floods and fires), and 'air conditioned.' This primitive air conditioning was accomplished by hauling large blocks of ice under the stage and blowing fans over them. I don't know how well the technique worked to cool down the interior of the grand theater, but they have certainly proven their claim of being fire proof. Of the more then twenty theaters that use to make up Manchester's theatre district, known as the "Great White Way," only the Palace Theatre has survived.

That's not to say that it's all been standing ovations and roses at the Palace Theatre. Once movies began to get popular, and especially after sound was added to cinema, less and less people went out for live entertainment. The Palace Theatre survived these years by becoming a movie house, but with its older sound system, it didn't do very well. Eventually it became an X-rated movie theater before finally shutting its doors.

Next, the theatre became classroom space for New Hampshire College, although it would not be long before the school, too, abandoned the building. After that, it was sometimes used as a warehouse. Anything that could be torn up and sold, was, and eventually, everything else left to decay.

Just before the curtains were about to close on the Palace Theatre forever, the building was saved by the Mayor of Manchester, at the time, Sylvio S. Dupuis, and a local lawyer by the name of John McLane. Between their inspired, massive fundraising campaign and several generous grants, the theatre was restored to its former glory and reopened its door in the mid 1970s.

Today the Palace Theatre is the center of Manchester's performing arts community, and is a wonderfully restored and rehabilitated 870-seat theatre. In fact, the place looks so good, that at least one of its original Vaudeville performers has come back to stay permanently. The old adage states that *all good theatres are haunted theatres* and the Palace is no exception to the rule.

A vaudeville actor, by the name of Will Cressy, who worked the stage at the Palace Theatre back in its early years, wants to make sure that his presence is known, and that everything is still running smoothly at the theatre he loved so much in life. Staffers at the theatre sometimes credit him as being The Palace's guardian angel, and think he may be the good luck charm that has helped the theatre get through a few disasters. Will Cressy is very much a welcome and a deeply-respected presence at the old theatre.

There is an old saying that *all good theatres are haunted*, and with the ghost of an old Vaudeville comedian hanging around, Manchester's historic Palace Theatre proves the rule correct.

A former marketing director became a believer in the ghost of Will Cressy one night while she was alone counting ticket stubs in the downstairs box office. As she looked down, silently counting the ticket sales to herself, a wave of cold air swept though the room. It got so cold, she was even able to see her breath when she breathed out. The marketing director was startled to feel a hand on her shoulder and someone breathing warmly on her neck. She hadn't heard anyone come down the stairs, but had been so focused on the sudden cold air that she just assumed it was another staffer, coming to tell her that the air conditioner was malfunctioning. A few moments went by and the person didn't say anything, just kept on breathing down her neck. When the woman turned around to confront the heavy breather, there was no one there.

A woman who was upstairs, at the same time her boss was getting up close and personal with a ghost, also felt the freezing cold air, but when she checked the heating and air conditioning system, all were working correctly.

The marketing director was intrigued by her strange encounter and started to ask around about the ghost. It was then that another staffer told her that everyone thought it was the ghost of Will Cressy, a regular performer at the Palace back when it first opened, who later died in Florida. The theatre's Artistic Director heard she was interested in the old legends about the theatre and told her this interesting story about a time that he was visited by the ghost. The man told her that he was going over a stack of bills on his desk one day, trying to decide what needed to be paid immediately and what could wait a few weeks. Tired of bending over the adding machine and account books, he decided to take a break and go to get some lunch. When he returned to his locked office, he found the bills had been shuffled around and a few of them tossed on the floor. Deciding that it must be the Palace Theatre's guardian angel trying to help him out, he decided to pay the bills left on the desk first, leave the rest until the proceeds came in from the next weeks' performances, and was able to get home early that day.

A few staffers and patrons have reported hearing keys jingling and the sound of footsteps when no one was there. Rarer still, but not unheard of, are the people who actually see the apparition of a man with a set of keys hooked over the belt loop of his jeans, that jingled as he walked. This may not be the spirit of Will Cressy; there is speculation that this man was a former manager at the theatre, and he's not ready to let go of his job title just yet.

The Home Coming

Melissa had had enough! Six years married to an abusive drug addict who couldn't hold down a job or keep from partying every night was six years too long in her book. To be honest, she was a little embarrassed to be in this position. She knew she really did love her husband, Gary, and that most of the time he was a wonderful father to their little girl. But after six very long years of making excuses for the things he did, Melissa was ready to admit defeat. She couldn't save Gary, she'd been a fool to even try, and it was time she start taking care of herself.

Gary was heart broken and angry when he was served with the divorce papers. He was terrified that it was Melissa's way to keep him away from the little girl he adored more than anything. He didn't care what she thought, he may not have been the best husband all of the time, but Gary knew he was a good daddy. When Gary was sober and drug-free, though, he didn't blame Melissa in the least. Gary was probably as amazed at how long his wife had stuck around as she was. If she wanted a divorce that bad, she could have it, but he'd be damned if a divorce would keep him from his little girl!

After a few months, it was done and the divorce was final. It got messy, for awhile, and Gary swore up and down that nothing, *nothing,* would keep him from seeing his daughter. Melissa supported him one hundred percent on this. It was never her intention to keep the little girl from the father she worshipped. Melissa just knew in her heart that they couldn't keep on waiting for the day when he'd get the help he so desperately needed. She even kind of hoped that the divorce would be the wakeup call Gary needed to help motivate him to go and get some help for his problems.

Unfortunately, Gary would never get the help he needed. Within six months of his divorce, he was dead, victim of an overdose that surprised no one. Melissa had been preparing for this day since she had first met Gary, and felt numb to the whole thing. She did her best to comfort her daughter. It was terrible that Gary was dead, but she and her daughter weren't, and they had to move on with their lives.

A year passed, and right around the anniversary of Gary's death, strange things began happening in the house where Melissa and her daughter now lived. It started with flickering lights, but within a week, things started to get flung around rooms, tossed by an unseen hand. Radios would start playing by themselves, cars wouldn't start, and doors flew open and slammed shut on their own. Cell phones stopped working the instant someone walked through the front door, even though they would instantly return to life as soon as they left Melissa's house. Their cat was so scared of the things that were going on, it ran outside and refused to come back into the house. Melissa had to start feeding it outside on the porch, or it would have starved before it came back inside to eat.

The activity never seemed to happen around Melissa's little girl, and she was thankful for that. But when her daughter was in the room with her, Melissa couldn't shake the feeling that someone was watching her daughter. It was as if someone was following in the little girls footsteps and constantly surrounding her. Her daughter seemed oblivious to whatever the presence was, so Melissa never mentioned it, fearing she would scare the girl over nothing.

Melissa started to worry that she was losing her mind. How could she tell that some unseen thing was following her daughter? And why didn't the thought terrify her like it should have?

One night, after hazy, half remembered dreams woke her, Melissa found herself awake but paralyzed. The air was alarmingly cold and her blanket had slipped off her as she slept, but she couldn't even move her arm to pull it back over her. Melissa felt exposed and vulnerable. She was completely unable to get to out of bed. She tried to turn to reach the lamp and turn on the lights, but couldn't even get her arms to move that short distance. She could see nothing above her; she had no idea how she was being held down. She shut her eyes, thinking maybe she was still asleep, and tried to will herself to wake up. With her eyes shut, she got the sense of her husband above her. She imagined him as just a dark outline, sitting on top of her and holding down her arms, trying desperately to get her to listen to the words he was saying, but she couldn't make them out. The jumble of syllables came out too fast, too low. It was like listening to a television turned to a station it didn't receive very well, playing one room over. She never could explain how, but after several minutes, even though she couldn't make out the words Gary was trying to speak to her, she got the idea of what he was trying to communicate.

"Oh, honey," Melissa breathed, not sure if this was real or just a very vivid dream "Of course I forgive you, of course you can always see your baby."

Suddenly, the weight holding her down was gone, and after that, all of the ghostly phenomena in the house stopped—although Melissa could not shake the feeling that her daughter was never alone in this world. Some nights, when she couldn't sleep, Melissa would have long conversations with her dead husband, finally saying all the things she wished she had said to him before.

The River Road Jogger

If you ever happen to find yourself on River Road around Halloween night, you'll probably be pretty surprised at all the people you see. Cars line the sides of the normally quiet residential street, with eager faces peering out into the night, as they sip hot chocolate, and await the chance of seeing Manchester's most well known, and probably least exciting, entity.

The River Road Jogger has been a Manchester landmark since he was first seen in the early 1970s. Since then, he has appeared, without fail, every Halloween night, between 1:45 and 2:20 in the morning. There have also been reports of him showing up, in that same half hour time frame, up to a week before or a week after the Halloween holiday.

The jogger is said to appear as an indistinct white mist, that slowly gains form as he runs down River Road. By the time he nears the end of his circuit, he is so plain to see that many people have, in fact, mistaken him for an actual living jogger. At least until they try to get his attention and are unable to, or he runs right through them and disappears!

The jogger looks straight forward as he runs, serious and engrossed in what he is doing, each year wearing the same red running shorts and a red sweatshirt. His graying hair suggests a man of age, unruffled by wind, and remaining dry even on the nights that it rains. His footsteps make no sound against the pavement, and, a few times, there has been snow on the road when the jogger passed by, and all witnesses say that he leaves not even one footprint in the slush.

People have said that they've tried shouting at the apparition, even running alongside him for a few minutes, but he takes no notice of them. When he completes the length of River Road he disappears until the Halloween season comes around the next year.

The River Road Jogger type of haunting is known by several different names. Sometimes it is referred to as an atmospheric or location-based haunting. It is also sometimes called a residual or repeat haunting. Basically, this ghost is like a movie that just keeps replaying the same scene over and over again. For whatever reason, this man left behind an echo of himself that will keep on doing the same thing, in the same spot, presumably, forever.

This stretch of River Road is visited yearly by a ghostly jogger.

The River Road Jogger is a little unusual because these types of hauntings tend to be created at scenes where there is a sudden explosive outpouring of negative energy. Replay hauntings often strike up at the scenes of particularly gruesome crimes, or places where families all die together. There are no known records of anything violent happening on River Road. There was no horrific hit and run accident involving a jogger, lets say, and not even an unsolved disappearance of one. People who have lived on the street for a long time have tried to see if it's a man any of them know—someone they recognize—but no one seems to recall a former neighbor who had a little bit of an exercise kick.

Very few people find this ghost particularly scary, and it's a Halloween tradition for a lot of folks to watch him make his yearly run. No one thinks he looks especially distressed as he takes his yearly jog up the winding residential street. He certainly doesn't appear to be running *away* from anything. As reliable as he is, the River Road Jogger is, if anything, maybe one of the most boring ghosts that Manchester has to offer, even if he is one of their best known. After all, how many times can you watch an uneventful jog up the street before it gets too old to be worth the trip?

Saint Anselm College

The ghost of a monk haunts the fourth floor of the Alumni Hall at prestigious Saint Anselm College. The only problem is, no one can seem to decide exactly how he got there!

Saint Anselm was founded in 1889 by the Benedictine Monks, a religious order that has been around for more then fifteen centuries. The school is one of the premier Catholic liberal arts schools in the country. It is ranked among the best colleges in the United States, appearing in *The Princeton Review's Best 345 Colleges* alongside Ivy league colleges like Yale and Harvard.

The building now known as Alumni Hall was the first building on the campus. Today, it is used as a woman's dorm and houses the administration offices. It is home to the schools most well known, and probably most mysterious ghost—though he is not the only ghost that upperclassman like to haze the incoming freshmen with. There are many other spirits that make their appearances in various spots around the Saint Anselm College campus, too.

It seems like everyone has heard a different reason why the monk is unable, or unwilling, to leave his post at Saint Anselm College. Some students swear by the story that this monk committed suicide in the fourth floor bathroom during an extreme crisis of faith, and that, as a suicide victim, he is doomed to forever walk the hallways where he died. There does seem to be something melancholy about the black-hooded figure. An offshoot of this story is that it was a janitor who committed suicide in the fourth floor bathroom after he saw the ghostly monk and no one would believe him.

Other people are equally as convinced that the fourth floor of the Alumni Hall was used as the area where they prepared the monks for burial when they died. This monk, they say, was somehow not given proper burial, and he walks the hallways in anguish, denied the comforts of heaven through no mistake of his own.

Yet even more people say that this monk died in the Alumni Hall itself, and his spirit is just lingering on in the last place his body was before death. That story tells us that the fourth floor of the building was used as an infirmary, and the monk got sick one day and died. Or, was it that he died simply of a heart attack and just happened to be in the Alumni Hall at that moment? What about a stroke; didn't he die of a stroke or brain embolism? There are about as many variations of this story as you can imagine.

There are still other stories telling that he fell down four flights of stairs and broke his neck. And, of course, there are those who say the monk was murdered, and that he will continue to haunt the building until his murderers are brought to justice.

Saint Anselm College Alumni Hall, the oldest building on campus and home to two spirits.

Yet another version of this story states that a fire raged through the Alumni Hall, and that the monk was either caught unaware and died in the blaze, or that he died fighting the fire, being a hero, and trying to save the building from being destroyed. He now patrols the hallways for eternity, keeping a careful eye out for other fires that might threaten the school he loved.

While the variety of stories about his origins may lead you to discount the haunting altogether, thinking it mere legend, there have been many, many witnesses to the things that go on at the Alumni Hall at night. Students and security guards alike have reported hearing ghostly footsteps, and eerie lights are sometimes seen through the windows, but when people go to investigate, no source to the lights can be found. This ghost is also often visible; his hooded form can be seen wandering the halls nightly. The hooded monk seems to like spending time in the girls bathroom. (But before you start worrying about immoral and lascivious monks at the school, keep in mind that this ghost most likely dates to a time where the college was a *boys only* facility.) At night, the bathroom doors swing open and shut on their own, the faucets run with water even when no one turns the handles, and some of the stalls in the fourth floor restroom are known to suddenly lock all by themselves.

One student, standing outside the building late one night, saw the hooded form of the monk pacing back and forth from one window to the next. The whole thing seemed pretty ordinary, until it occurred to this student that not only was no one supposed to be in the building, but those windows were not even in the same room—they were separated by a wall that the monk upstairs didn't even seem to notice. Campus security, and even Manchester police, have been called to investigate strange noises and lights coming from the building, but they have never found an Earthly intruder causing the problems there.

Statue of Saint Benedict at Saint Anselm College.

Many of the Saint Anselm security guards refuse to go into the building alone at night, and there is a high turnover rate in the cleaning people who get stuck mopping the floors in the Alumni Hall.

While we may not know who this monk was, or how he died, there is little doubt that he is a permanent fixture at the college. He has been reported for at least fifty years. The school administrators may dislike his presence, and do all they can to quell the ghost stories, but students have come to expect unusual occurrences in the Alumni Hall, especially when they are on the fourth floor.

There are at least four other known entities that have made Saint Anselm College their home, although many of them are as shrouded in mystery as the monk who wanders around the fourth floor. No one is exactly sure why Saint Anselm College is so haunted, or if there is a connection between the ghosts. It seems almost as though as soon as you walk out of the area of one haunting, you've walked right into the territory of another spirit. In fact, one of these spirits lives right next door to the ghostly monk, in the attached building that students refer to as "The Streets."

This second ghost at Saint Anselm College is that of a former student. Legend says that the girl committed suicide there while she was a student, possibly over a love affair gone bad—when her lover left her because she was pregnant, or possibly because she was pregnant and lost her baby. This ghost seems to have an adverse effect on electrical equipment that is brought into the building. Cell phones get only static, even if they work fine the rest of the time, and televisions turn on and off by themselves when she is around. At night, while students lay in their beds, they watch unseen hands move ceiling tiles around, and sometimes furniture as well. In more violent moods, this ghost is known to toss around text books.

The dorms at the haunted Alumni Hall; televisions and cell phones are effected by the presence of the spirit of a young girl here.

The Saint Joan of Arc girls dorm is also haunted. No one knows who the ghost was in life, but that building also suffers from cell phone interference. Students in this dorm sometimes have to turn their cell phones off as soon as they walk through the door, otherwise they ring and ring and ring, but there is never anyone on the other line. Sometimes instead of static, they pick up a painful metallic screeching sound. Locking a door at the Saint Joan of Arc dorms is no guarantee that they will stay locked, or shut, and there are some extreme cold spots that float around the building and seem to gravitate towards gatherings of students.

Saint Anselm College is located outside of the downtown area of Manchester and is surrounded by woods. A headless ghost is sometimes seen walking through these woods, most often between the Dominic Hall men's dorms and the haunted girls' Saint Joan of Arc dorms. Sometimes the figure is described as wearing a monk's robe, but other people who have seen the ghost say it is impossible to tell if he is wearing one, or not. The figure appears shrouded in mist and missing his head. He doesn't give much notice to the students he sometimes comes upon, although walking up on a headless man in the woods certainly gives them a fright. Some people say that if you talk to the ghost, or try to touch it, it instantly turns into indistinct mist and dissipates on the wind.

These dorms are in the area haunted by an headless apparition
whose origins are unknown.

The path that the headless ghost walks, runs very close to the small graveyard located on Saint Anselm College campus where several priests from the school have been buried. Students say that, sometimes, there are glittering lights in the graveyard at night that disappear when they go to investigate their source. Occasionally, there are the sounds of voices raised in prayer, or chanting softly, even when you can see with your own two eyes that there is no one there.

Close up of graves in Saint Anselm College Cemetery; some of the Fathers buried here date all the way back to the 1800s.

The haunted cemetery at Saint Anselm College.

Samuel

As usual, the owner of the suspected haunted house had let himself be driven nearly crazy before giving in and calling Raven Duclos to come and investigate the problems at the house. The man had been living with an increasingly unhappy spirit for months before anyone could get in there and find out what was going on.

Things started out innocently enough. Lights flickered, sometimes there were thumps and rattles with no explanation, or rooms would seem a little colder then those directly next to them. But after a few weeks, things took a turn for the worse. Figurines were hurtled off shelves, smashed against walls, and entire stacks of books would be knocked over.

The homeowner couldn't begin to imagine what was going on. It seemed obvious to him that there was a ghost in the house, but how could that be? He was friendly with the previous owners of the home, and he was sure they would have told him, at least in passing, if there had ever been anything that happened like this before. Could a house suddenly just become haunted for no reason? Visitors to the house sometimes witnessed the ghostly problems the homeowner was enduring, but for the most part, the activity was limited to just him and his possessions.

When the crew from Ghost Quest arrived, they were able to asses the situation and tell the man what was going on. His home was haunted by the spirit of an African American man who gave his name as just *Samuel*. Samuel and his sister had been attacked and killed in the area hundreds of years before. The two bodies were hidden, and their murderers got away with the crime. In fact, no one had even realized a crime had been committed. The bodies were never found, and Samuel's parents never knew what had become of the siblings. Because this happened at a time when racism was still alive and well in America, no one paid much attention when the young man and woman were reported missing. The question of what had happened to their children would haunt Samuel's parents for the rest of their days.

Samuel was not willing to move on until someone knew what had happened to him and his sister. He was angry that there could be no retribution against the killers who had died themselves a long, long time ago. The reason why the homeowner was being targeted by the ghost was because, even though he didn't know it, he had some latent abilities to sense the dead that most people seemed to lack. Samuel had been desperately trying to get the man to hear his story, and finally lashed out in frustration when the man was unable to understand him.

Once Samuel's tale was known, it seemed to appease the ghost. Nothing else was broken by the fury of unseen hands, and things returned back to normal in the house. Raven says that, many times, she has seen spirits act out, either from frustration, or just to bring attention to themselves. Much like the ghost of Avery at Bob Shaw's Sub Shop, if you acknowledge them and try to listen to them, they will usually leave, or at least stop breaking things.

Strange Happenings on Rock Rimmon

Rock Rimmon is an enormous outcropping of rock, nearly 300 feet long and 150 feet wide, that rises up hundreds of feet above the city. The rock is composed of gneiss and is something of a geological oddity in the area. Its unique geological makeup has even been written about in texts as far away as Germany. The rock dates back to the days before man, when glaciers carved out the sandy plateau that the city would later spring from, leaving this chunk of gneiss behind.

It seems as though the people of Manchester have always linked it to odd or creepy happenings. In a poem published in the August 15, 1915 edition of the now defunct Manchester newspaper, *The Amoskeag Bulletin*, the rock was described as being "like some proud tombstone of the mighty dead."

Like several rocks and cliffs in New Hampshire, it was given the name of Rock Rimmon, seemingly in honor of the more biblically famous stone near the city of Jerusalem, although in some earlier texts this name has been corrupted to Rock Raymond, or Raymon. No one is sure who exactly named the rock, although it is known that it has been called that for at least 200 years, and most likely, quite a bit longer then that.

As is true for most of the area in and around Manchester, it was once owned by the Amoskeag Manufacturing Company. After owning it for a hundred years or so, the company decided that the Rock truly belonged to the people of Manchester. They donated the rock and the land around it, altogether some nearly forty-three acres, with the condition that it would be turned into a park for all residents to enjoy.

There have always been stories about the rock. It has been known as a *lovers leap* for a long time; it's a well-known destination for rock climbers around New England, offering a view from the top that looks out more then five miles across the city on a clear day. It has become a popular party spot with Manchester teens, despite it's haunted reputation, and the accidents there that have claimed several lives over the years.

One of the earliest stories about Rock Rimmon dates back to before the American Revolution, from the time when the white settlers first came to what would become known as Manchester. One of these settlers was a young Englishman who was known by the unlikely name of Alberto. Alberto, who was of noble lineage, came to the newly forming colony to help educate the native Penacook Indians. He found one young native American maiden to be a particularly apt student, and, as time went by, he fell in love with her. Despite the tension this caused between the native tribes people and the young teacher, the young native American girl soon began to love him back. Her father was a great chieftain among the Penacook, and many young warrior braves felt that Alberto was besmirching her reputation, and thus ruining any chance she had of getting married to one of her own people.

Rock Rimmon and the land around it were given to Manchester to create a park for the citizens of the city to enjoy.

One evening, Alberto asked the maid to meet him atop the rock so they could watch the sunset together. From the top of the rock, the two lovers could see two very different villages spread out below them. On one side, they saw the native American village where she had been born and raised; on the other, the beginnings of the City of Manchester. Alberto was dressed winsomely in the traditional English hunting outfit that was all the rage at that time, and the maiden was wearing a beautiful white dress cut in the English style, that had been a gift from him. The young maiden had braided fresh water pearls into her raven black hair. Alberto clasped her hands to his heart and told her his exciting news. He would be leaving New Hampshire and taking a boat back to his home in England. But he did not plan on traveling alone. Alberto said he had told his parents about his love for her, and that he wished for her to travel with him to England as his bride. They would be married shortly after arriving. Their journey would begin the next day at dawn. Alberto told her to gather a few reminders from home to bring with her, and that she should meet him at dawn on top of Rock Rimmon. There, they would begin their life together. Although she would be sad to leave behind the only life she had ever known, the maiden knew in her heart that she loved Alberto and could not live without him by her side. She accepted his proposal eagerly.

Unfortunately, neither Alberto nor his bride-to-be knew that, for some time, the young men of the native American tribe had taken to following the couple so they could be sure nothing improper was occurring on the couple's walks. When the young warriors heard this plan, they became enraged. When the couple came to the fork in the mountain pass, they kissed, briefly, and parted ways, so Alberto could see to their travel plans and his bride could go to her village to tell her father her news. As soon as the maiden turned the corner, Alberto was attacked and killed by the young men of her village.

The young woman was still in her father's long-house arguing with him when the men arrived with her lover's scalp to prove to her what they had done. When she saw the shock of her lovers hair, she knew they were telling her the truth. She gave an eerie wail and sank to her knees, frozen—as if made of stone. The people from the tribe encircled her and tried to reason or comfort her, but the young maiden re-mained frozen in place. They began to talk of curses and were afraid to try to move her. As the sun started to rise, so did the grief stricken girl. She rose to her feet, her white dress streaked with dirt, and started to walk towards the summit of the rock. The tribes peo-ple were to terrified to try to stop her.

When she reached the top of Rock Rimmon, she whispered to the wind, "I told thee at dawn I would meet thee. I will be thy spirit bride."

With a last look down at her village, and that of the white settlers, the girl flung herself off the rock. Days later, when word got around as to what had hap-pened, the bodies of the two lovers were retrieved, and together the native Americans and the encroaching white settlers buried them, side by side, along the banks of the Merrimack River. Some versions of this story say that the maiden's name was Rimmon, or Raymond (which seems as unlikely as her lover being named Alberto, but who knows?) and that the rock was named in her honor, as well as to give solace to her father.

Do ghosts walk these paths in the woods surrounding haunted Rock Rimmon?

Although the story says that she was given a proper burial and laid to rest beside Alberto as if she were his wife, the lovelorn girl does not seem to rest easy with her lover beside her. Her white-clad figure can often be seen making the lonely walk to the top of the Rock, or pacing along its summit. Sometimes she stands so still, it is as if she is made of rock herself, and many climbers have thought she was a statue put in place as a monument atop the rock—until they see her disappear.

But the young native American maiden is not the only ghost of Rock Rimmon. Local lore tells us that, later, after her suicide, things began to go badly for the native tribe. They had managed to gather a large amount of wealth by trading furs with the white settlers, but as they prospered, so did the city. Soon the city began to creep closer and closer to their village, and the native Americans knew it was time to move and find better hunting grounds. Not wanting to leave their wealth or their cache of weapons to be found by either the white man or the neighboring tribes who they had long warred with, the chieftain of the tribe hid all their belongings in a cave on Rock Rimmon. He sealed the entrance so it would not be noticeable to anyone coming by. Years later, there was a landslide on the rock, and the entrance was lost to even the people who had placed their treasures there.

Geologically speaking, it is unlikely that this story is anything more then myth—there has never been evidence found of a cave or landslide on the slopes of Rock Rimmon. But that certainly hasn't stopped people from talking about, and dreaming about, a pile of gold and jewels hidden on the rock. Many would-be treasure hunters report being thrown off the chase by the spirit of a great Native American chief who staunchly guards the treasure in the hopes that some day his people will come back for it and use it to remove the people that took their lands.

Adding to the mystery surrounding Rock Rimmon is the non-ghostly, but still peculiar tale, of the lost profile of the rock. In 1925, the State Forestry Commissioner at the time, John Corliss, discovered the face of a native American naturally built into the rock, much like the famous profile in the north on Franconia's Notch that drew tourists from all over the world, until it collapsed just a few years ago. The face was said to be quite distinct, even easier to see then the famous Old Man in the Mountain, and it caused quite a stir. Once it was pointed out, it was so obvious to see, that no one could explain why it had never been noticed before. The story was published in several newspapers around the state, along with photos of the Old Man in the Mountain. Compared side by side, it was obvious how much better the profile of the Manchester mountain man looked. The face was photographed many times and was plain to see from a certain spot below the rock. The Parks Commission began plans to build viewing platforms, and to start advertising in travel magazines—the hope being that the Old Man of Rock Rimmon would soon draw visitors away from the north, and bring them into Manchester. Without warning, all the plans were dropped;

no one could, or would, explain why. Stranger still, no one could seem to find the face anymore! No rock-slides were reported, and the noise from a collapse, if one had happened, should have drawn the attention of local residents, if nothing else. Although photos of the naturally occurring formation survive, the location where one needs to stand to view the phenomenon has been obscured by time. All in all, the face that was there—and then wasn't—is probably the strangest of all the stories surrounding Rock Rimmon.

Special Rock Rimmon Warning!

You should think twice before lacing up your hiking boots and heading off to Rock Rimmon to search for ghosts, Indian treasure, or the lost profile. It is an extremely bad idea to try ghost hunting at Rock Rimmon, especially at night, if you're not familiar with the terrain—and ghosts have nothing to do with just how dangerous it is. While there are a few easy trails to the top, they are lined with sharp blades of glass from broken bottles and littered with the effluvia of years of teen partying. The Rock has been climbed by famous, and not so famous, mountaineers, and is considered a pretty demanding climb. Firefighter recruits from all over New Hampshire even practice rescue missions on the rock. Although a popular party spot for high school kids, the Rock has had more then its share of accidents and deaths over the years. It's not a place to go ghost hunting on a whim. The list of its victims range from an eight-year-old boy, who got off comparatively lightly with back and leg injuries, to a seventy-five-year-old woman who either fell or jumped from the precipice. One eighteen-year-old man fell without warning, while two friends watched on—the three young men had climbed the rock to watch the sunset. It was only a few days after his eighteenth birthday that the young man lost his life.

Even experienced mountain climbers have gotten into trouble on Rock Rimmon. In 1992, a young man who described himself as "not a novice climber" had to be rescued by firefighters when he got stuck coming down the slope. The Manchester newspaper, the *Union Leader*, reported that the young man told authorities that he had climbed all over Rock Rimmon, many times, and couldn't understand how he had gotten lost.

Because of the excessive noise from parties and the danger the Rock poses, residents in the area teamed up with Manchester police in 2001 in a "Take Back the Rock" campaign, to keep people off the dangerous summit. During this time, underage drinkers from as far away as Vermont, Boston, and upstate New York were caught on Rock Rimmon—some of them telling police about the strange lady dressed in white they saw walking around up top.

Rock Rimmon, as seen from Rock Rimmon Park.

Man's Best Friend

A lot of hauntings happen when someone dies, and instead of passing on to whatever it is that comes next, the deceased decides to stay on Earth to watch over friends and family. These souls sometimes come to warn their loved one of a coming disaster, or even just to provide comfort in times of need. More rarely, but certainly not unheard of, these souls belong to peoples' pets, important family members in their own right, that sometime stay on after death, unable to leave behind the owners they adored so much in life. If spirits of people are sometimes seen, why not pets? Who could ever be more loyal to you then your beloved golden retriever, or the Siamese cat you've shared your life with for the past fifteen years?

Paranormal investigators aren't usually surprised when they get EVPs from a haunted house that has captured the sound of a ghostly dog barking, or the meows of a spirit cat. One woman, in California, recently started a group whose sole mission is to investigate animal hauntings, since, for phenomena that is so well documented, there is so little that is actually known about it.

One of the most famous ghost stories in the entire history of hauntings is that of Gef, the talking mongoose. The case occurred in the 1930s on the Isle of Man, just off the coast of Great Britain. It is one of those stories that still captures peoples' imaginations and causes controversy. Even today, people argue over whether Gef was a ghost, the only known animal poltergeist, or an amazingly elaborate, if somewhat ridiculous, hoax.

The Irving family was at the center of the strange story involving the creature they came to call Gef. The family started to hear chattering noises coming from their attic one day and reasoned that a squirrel or rat had gotten stuck in there; in a few days, if it couldn't get out on its own, someone would have to go up there and help it. Within that time, the animal started to talk. First it just mindlessly repeated whatever words the Irving family said to it, but after a week or so, it could converse fluently with the family. The creature told them that he was a mongoose and that his name was Gef. The creature gave them an exact date of birth and said he had originally come from New Delhi.

As wild as all this seems, there was a man on the island who had released several mongooses, possibly from India, on the island to try and curb the rabbit population that was eating all of his crops. It was not entirely out of the realm of possibility, therefore, that there could be an Indian mongoose living in Great Britain.

Several people outside of the Irving family heard Gef speak, too. One man was even threatened by the animal. Gef was able to make a believer out of many people by spying on the Irving's neighbors and coming back to tell the family things that the family could never have known. Needless to say, a lot of what he repeated made Gef none to popular with the Irving's neighbors. The neighbors also complained of strange animal noises at the times when it would seem that Gef would have been spying on them. A couple people took pictures of a mongoose running wild on the Irving property—which Gef complained about—but, of course, even a picture of a mongoose doesn't prove that it was a *talking* mongoose.

Soon enough, the press caught wind of what was happening in the otherwise quiet town, and the media descended on the family. People flocked from all over the world hoping to get a glimpse of the weird creature, and the famous psychic researcher and author, Harry Price, came to investigate the case.

Gef and the Irving family lived on the farm together for ten years without any one ever being able to prove the strange story one way or another. After the family moved, a new farmer took up residence in the house, and after a few years, shot something that he described as a strange mongoose-like animal that people generally take to mean Gef. One of the Irving daughters is still alive today and she refuses to say anything about the talking mongoose that her family lived with for so many years.

Of course, Gef is not a typical haunting, just as he is not your typical poltergeist, or a typical *anything* for that matter. There are many more average, believable accounts of everyday people interacting with their pets after the animal has passed on. Ghost dogs will usually still respond to their masters' commands, cats return to their favorite places, and things continue on for them much as it did when they were alive. It would seem that the bonds we create with our animals is not so easily broken, and continues on, long past death. The following are a few short tales of animals who have stayed on after death. They're sure to make you think twice next time you see your cat gleefully playing with, what looks to be, nothing at all.

No Bedtime for Buddy

Shannon babysat often for her neighbor's three kids, even though they loved to freak her out with their scary stories and the imaginary ghost they said lived under their beds. They were good kids, but she had never seen little kids so drawn to the macabre as they were. They loved stories with occult elements and begged to be allowed to watch monster movies when they played them on television.

While reading them bedtimes stories, Shannon felt a small row of teeth bite down gently on her bare foot. With a little yelp, she sat up quickly and tucked her feet under her. When she looked down, she had to laugh at herself. It was just the kids' little Jack Russell terrier, Buddy, who was probably the most harmless creature on Earth. Buddy, it seemed, was ready for playtime—not for bedtime.

"Uh, oh," Shannon said as a second, more likely possibility occurred to her, "when was Buddy let outside last?"

The oldest of the three kids gave her an odd look and told her that they didn't have the dog any longer. Shannon insisted that they obviously did. Then the child told her that Buddy had been hit by a car last week. At first, she thought the kids were trying to scare her again, and threatened to punish them for making up such an awful story, but when Shannon saw the tears well up in their little eyes she knew they were telling her the truth.

When the children's parents came home from the party they had been attending, Shannon asked them, too. The father confirmed that Buddy was buried out in the back garden. He told her that he, too, had seen the ghost of the dog, but he was hoping that Buddy wouldn't appear to the kids, who were very upset after he died and were just starting to get over his death.

The Wheel of Misfortune

It's not much of a stretch to imagine a cat returning to its favorite sunning window, or a dog returning faithfully to his master, but how about a gerbil from beyond the grave? One woman told the tale of how, after her daughter's pet gerbil had a fatal run-in with the family cat, the spirit of the little animal made nightly visits to its cage. The first night, when her daughter woke her up telling her that the exercise wheel in the gerbils cage was turning by itself, the woman didn't think too much of it; she told her daughter that it was just a dream and to go back to bed. By the third night, everyone in the house had seen and heard the wheel turning on its own. It was undeniable—something was still using the gerbil wheel, and what else could it be but the gerbil that had just died? The family decided to keep the animals cage set up and untouched so he could still enjoy it. The nightly visits lasted for six months, then abruptly stopped.

...And the Cat Came Back, It Couldn't Stay Away...

Jeanine has always kept cats as pets. She likes to joke that she'd planned on becoming a crazy cat lady when older. Even with all the pets, she felt an extra connection with her calico cat, Fern. She'd had Fern since she was a college student. She had found the animal, half starved and covered in cuts from fighting, cringing in an alleyway one day. The cat was so close to death, it didn't even fight her when she wrapped it up in her coat and snuck it back into her dorm room.

Luckily, Jeanine's roommates took pity on her, and expecting that the cat wouldn't make it, they agreed to help keep the animal secret and nurse it back to health. It took time, but eventually Fern recovered, and by then, no one wanted to bring her down to the shelter. It took some effort, but Jeanine was able to keep the cat with her all through college.

After that, the two were inseparable; Jeanine actually started 'collecting' cats just so Fern would have some companionship while she was at work. But Fern maintained a special place in the house, no matter how many new cats were brought in. Fern was the only one of Jeanine's cats that was allowed in her bedroom, and Fern slept with her every night.

The years went by, and Fern developed a lot of problems as she aged. She went through one surgery after another, and was on a regiment of pills that were impossible to get the cat to take. The vet kept telling Jeanine it couldn't go on like this forever. There would come a time when she wouldn't be doing this for Fern; she'd be forcing the cat to keep on going for herself. It broke Jeanine's heart to do it, but of course, the day finally came when there was nothing left that could be done for the geriatric cat, and she had to be put down. Jeanine was inconsolable.

That night, as Jeanine lay down to sleep, she heard the creak of her bedroom door as it slowly opened. Before she get up to see what had opened the door, Jeanine felt the small pressure of cat paws on her back and felt the animal circling as it found a comfortable spot to fall asleep. Jeanine knew that some day she'd find a cat to replace Fern, but she wasn't ready for one of cats to try and take over the position of alpha cat, so soon. When she rolled over to push the cat aside, she found that there was no animal there. It was then that she realized it must have been Fern trying to comfort her in the only way he could. For the next few nights, Jeanine felt the ghost cat come to her bed and take up its usual spot in the blankets.

A Long Journey Home

The Gilson family treated their old basset hound the way some families treat their kids. If they went on vacation, they brought back a t-shirt for the dog.

When Christmas rolled around each year, they had the dog's picture taken for the front of their holiday cards. They threw birthday parties for the dog, complete with doggy birthday cake, and let the animal sleep with them in their beds. Their answering machine message had their dog barking out a greeting to anyone who called the house and got the machine.

When the dog went missing for several days and no sign was seen of him, they knew that something bad must have happened. He would have come home, hell or high water, if he had been able too. After a few months went by, they felt that they shouldn't hold out more hope for the dog's return. They wondered if maybe he had been hit by a car, and the driver was too embarrassed to admit what had happened, or maybe someone had taken their beloved family pet.

They packed up the dog's toys and dog bed and put the things up in the attic where they wouldn't stumble across them accidentally, bringing back the pain of losing the pet they had cherished so much. The family also devised a new answering machine message. It seemed a little morbid, and not terribly polite, to have the phone answered by a dog who was most likely dead.

The first time they played back the newly recorded message they could still hear their dog barking away on the tape. Figuring that the tape was old and was causing some sort of distortion, they headed out to buy a brand new tape for the answering machine. No matter how many times they recorded over and over the message, each time, when played back, their words were obscured by the sound of a dog barking. A dog that sounded exactly like *their* dog on the old phone message. That's when the family knew for sure that something fatal had befallen the dog, but he had still found his way back home.

The Youth Detention Center

Aimee didn't know why she had agreed to go along with her brother and his friends when they said they wanted to explore the infamous abandoned building in the woods on the Youth Detention Center property. First off, and most importantly, it was trespassing, and the Center wasn't known for passing it off lightly when they caught someone doing it. More then a few of Aimee's friends had been brought home in police cars when they went out hunting for the ghost. Secondly . . . well, the stories about the place were creepy enough to give her nightmares. Did she really want to experience a haunting herself?

Located on the outskirts of Manchester, surrounded by woods and fields knee-high with crab grass, it was no picnic just getting to the center. Especially when you had to worry about the constant police patrols! Aimee knew that, even now, the center was in the process of being rebuilt. She knew that, on the property, there were several buildings that had largely been abandoned as the needs of the center have changed over the years and the new facilities are completed. Of course, like many abandoned buildings in such places, every teenager in town just *knew* they had to be haunted.

One building in particular had several scary stories associated with it. The fact that it was more securely boarded up and patrolled then the other empty buildings, only added fuel to the fire. If this otherwise average brick building surrounded by woods was more heavily guarded, Aimee reasoned, there must be a reason for it. It was the type of adventure that was right up her brother's alley. With their mom out and his friends over telling scary stories, there was no one there to stop him when he suddenly decided they needed to go and investigate the ghost for themselves.

This is the no trespassing sign at the front gates of Manchester's Youth Detention Center. Always get permission before visiting a haunted site yourself.

At first, Aimee had tried to reason with him. If every door and window were boarded over by several layers of plywood, and any possible crack or crevice had been sealed, then how did everyone know the place was haunted? Who broke *in* to a place like that anyway?

The construction of the new buildings at the Youth Detention Center has left many of the older ones empty and just ripe for haunting.

But even as he said it, Aimee knew that none of those facts kept people from exploring. It seemed like everyone at school knew someone—an older brother, a cousin, *some*one—who claimed to have made the trek out into the woods to catch the ghost at some point. These trespassers brought back odd tales of bizarre humming noises, that gave listeners instant

migraines, coming from the secured building, and other noises as well—laughing, gibbering nonsense, all tinged with a hint of madness that pours from the building even when you can tell that all of the boards and locks are in place and that no one could possibly be inside. There are, of course, those people who claim to have brought their crowbars and removed the plywood that was stopping them from entering. Most are instantly frightened off by an increase in the noises and a haunting dim light that roams the hallways as if looking for a way out.

Aimee didn't know what she was more scared of, catching a ghost, or getting caught herself by the police.

After getting lost a third time, Aimee started to wonder if they could even find the place, never mind worrying about what they would do when they got there! But luck wasn't on her side that night. Not only did they stumble upon the building, her brother had been smart enough to bring a crowbar with him. It took plenty of work from all three boys, but they finally created an opening large enough for them all to squeeze through. As soon as they entered the basement, Aimee couldn't shake the feeling that something just wasn't right. As they walked down the hallway to the first floor stairs, her worst fears were confirmed. Materializing without warning at the bottom of the stairs, a smoky white mist started to gather. Aimee begged the boys to turn around, but they only laughed at her and assured her that all the dust they were kicking up was the source of the deepening cloud. They took her aside into a room in the basement and tried to get her to calm down. She tried frantically to make them realize how petrified she felt.

Couldn't they see that something here just wasn't right?!

The boys kept on reassuring her and asking her to walk back into the hallway, pointing out that, by this time, all the dust would have settled. Aimee wasn't buying the dust theory, but she knew full well that she had to leave the basement room eventually—one way or another. Lining hands, the four teens walked back into the hallway. Now the mist blocking the stairs was so thick it looked dark gray, and the light of their sole flashlight couldn't penetrate through to the other side. The four teens clutched at each other and a loud banging started up at the base of the stairs. Each thud reverberated in their chests and made their ears ring. It almost sounded as though something impossibly heavy was walking down the old wooden stairs, obscured by the gathering mist. There was no more discussion; without a word they all fled, convinced that something was pursuing them through the dirty gray fog.

The Party
That Never Ends

Raven Duclos is a professional psychic and ghost hunter living and working in Manchester. You can read an interview with her at the end of this book where she talks about how she got started in the ghost business, as well as some of her adventures. During my interviews with her, I asked her to tell me about the most remarkable haunting she personally had ever investigated. This is the story she told.

A woman named Andrea, who was the owner of an unused building on Lake Street in Manchester, called the Ghost Quest offices and asked if she and her team of parapsychologists would come and take a look at her property. It had formerly been the site of a gentleman's club, but had been left empty for ten years or more. Raven was told by the owner that, over the years, many people had complained to her about the odd things that they heard and felt while in the building. She was having trouble getting the place rented or sold.

Intrigued by the story she'd been told, Raven made arrangements to view the property the next day. She, and her team, were not disappointed. Raven described the place as having a chaotic energy, unlike anything she'd ever experienced before. They all heard noises, and got many of them on tape—people talking and a piano playing. All in all, there was a kind of party atmosphere that was belied by the strange aura surrounding the building. Raven said she had the sense that the spirits, and there were definitely many, many ghosts in this once house of ill repute, were worried that she was there to try to convince them to leave. There was a high concentration of energy in this one place, and Raven knew that this was much more then a simple haunting.

She took many photographs while walking through the building, and no one was surprised to find a plethora of orbs dotting the pictures when they were developed. These orbs are the most commonly photographed ghosts, and there were literally dozens of them in this building. There was a piano left on the second floor, presumably the same one that the ghostly musician had been playing for them, and the photographs Raven took seemed to confirm that a lot of energy was focused around this instrument. They also got some disturbing pictures of something peering out of a second floor window at them as they left the building. Additionally, there was a large concentration of orbs haunting the third floor, for no reason anyone could explain.

Raven returned to the building a few days later, this time at night, to continue her research. During the second visit, she said the energies in the building were much more negative, and much stronger, then during the day. Raven's daughter, also a much-experienced psychic, was there, and frantically, she called out to her mother that she felt like she was being led up the stairs. Raven told her not to panic and took several photos of her daughter walking up the stairs. Later on, when the pictures were developed, it was easy to see the transparent figure of a man waking up the stairs in front of her daughter, even though, at the time, everyone agreed there was no one there.

The ghost hunters decided that their next step should be to hold a channeling session in the building. They were able to communicate very freely with the spirit of a woman, who identified herself as Joan. While they questioned Joan, and tried to find out why these ghosts were lingering on at this place, Raven felt like she could barely breathe—thanks to the three spirits that crowded around her. Later on, they were able to get photographic evidence of the three spirits Raven had sensed standing with her.

Raven felt very strongly that the presences in the building were not going to leave on their own, and she also felt that they were very dangerous spirits to have hanging around; so with the owner's permission, and the help of her crew, they cleansed the building and asked the spirits to leave.

Valley Street Cemetery

The City of Manchester boasts several historic, and a few not so historic, cemeteries. So it should probably come as no surprise to anyone that at least one of them, is purported to be haunted. Valley Street Cemetery, at twenty acres, is the largest green space in the city, and is listed on the National Registrar of Historic Places. Like many of Manchester's historic places, the land for the burial ground was donated to the city by the Amoskeag Manufacturing Company and, though you probably couldn't tell by looking at it as it is today, Valley Street Cemetery began life commonly called, "Manchester's Garden Cemetery," when it first opened in 1841. Garden cemeteries were extremely popular in New England at this time, and Valley Street Cemetery was the epitome of what the genteel Victorian loved about the style.

The twenty acres were a carefully landscaped haven of sculptured gardens, hidden walking paths, picturesque gazebos, and carriage lanes that wound around and over the gurgling brook that ran through the center of the plot of land. The Amoskeag's Machine Shop produced the ornate wrought-iron fence that still encircles the graveyard today, and hundreds of trees were planted throughout the area. The cemetery quickly became the number one destination in the city for picnics and romantic carriage rides—it was easy to forget that this was a place for the dead!

The Currier Gates; the main entrance to the very haunted Valley Street Cemetery.

The cemetery hosts, among many others, two New Hampshire governors, sixty Civil War soldiers, a handful of veterans from the Revolutionary War, at least one fighter hailing from the French and Indian War, scores of former Manchester mayors, as well as the descendants of the city's first founding families.

The people that the historic society is less willing to brag about are the many poor people who were buried in paupers' graves in the northwest section of the cemetery, or the unfortunate inhabitants of the northeastern corner of the grounds. During the 1850s, when Manchester suffered a series of cholera outbreaks, the victims of the disease were buried here in mass gravesites, at midnight, with no loved ones or funerals to see them on their way.

These two sections of the cemetery have a long history of hauntings, probably from spirits who are unhappy with the way they were buried and forgotten. There are few to no tombstones to mark the resting spots of these people, and it is impossible to tell who might still be hanging around their final resting spots. They manifest their presence with cold spots and faint murmurings that people who have experienced the sounds describe as mournful and sad. Many visitors to the cemetery have described feeling as if they were being watched. A few have even said they felt hands on their shoulders, as if someone was trying to turn them around to get them to look at them, but there is no one there when they turn to look.

VALLEY
CEMETERY

FOUNDED 1841

listed in the

NATIONAL REGISTER
OF HISTORIC PLACES

by the United States
Department of the Interior
2004

Plaque on the Currier Gates designating this as a historic site.

The ghosts in this section of the cemetery seem to crave attention, but do not have enough energy or form to do anything to really attract someone's attention. Their voices are barely audible, and usually don't even show up on audio recordings taken in the cemetery. The most they are able to manifest is, sometimes, just the faintest smell of flowers.

These ghosts are sad, but not particularly scary. The greatest nuisance to Valley Street Cemetery aren't these faceless, forgotten ghosts—it is time and vandals who have taken the largest toll. The ground's glory days are long past. Now the stream, that decorated horse carriages use to gallop over, is mixed with the city's sewage and covered over, though the stench is not so easily contained. There is a rusted-out sewage overflow pipe marring the valley that helped give the cemetery, and the street it's located on, its name. The thirteen private mausoleums, most belonging to Manchester's founding families, have been covered in graffiti that is costly and, in some cases, impossible to repair. The serenity of the cemetery is spoiled by broken tombstones and rusting, incomplete, iron fences.

However, despite the murmurings of the dead and the air of disrepair, the grounds are still a treat for visitors. They still contains historic trees, many dating back to the 1800s, various beautiful headstones that bring gravestone rubbers from all over the northeast, and some interesting architecture. So, in 2002, the Friends of Valley Cemetery, a group of concerned local citizens, teamed up with the city to try to restore the grounds to their former beauty. The work is time consuming and costly, the money raised by private donations and fundraising events like the annual Strawberry Festival that is held by the Friends of Valley Street Cemetery on the grounds each June.

As slow as the work has been, still a great deal of progress has been made in the past four years. The large Currier Gates have been removed, repaired, and repainted. A generous grant from the United States Forestry Service, that was matched dollar for dollar by the City of Manchester, has saved many of the 365 historic trees and put them in a better position to survive another couple of hundred years.

Pathways have been reworked, spray paint sand blasted away, and fences restored and rebuilt. However, at least one of the cemetery's permanent residents seems to be none to happy with all the work being done and the influx of visitors it's brought to Valley Street.

The Frederick Smyth mausoleum is one of the grandest in Valley Street Cemetery; it looms up over the land with an imposing view of the central valley, with tall straight Grecian pillars and stately marble construction. The quiet solidity of the Smyth Mausoleum has become the focus of a great deal of paranormal activity. Two spirits haunt the area surrounding the tomb, locked in battle, and they seem to be getting only more and more active as time goes on.

Three historic grave markers at Valley Street Cemetery. An amateur photographer snapped a photo of what she thinks is a ghost at this spot, early in 2006.

The ghost most often felt and heard is that of a young woman who lingers near the doorway of the mausoleum. She is preceded by the scent of an old-fashioned floral perfume, and is known to be very protective of the living people that come near what is, presumably, her final resting spot. And those people just might need her protection. The second ghost haunting the area near Smyth's mausoleum is an angry older man who brings a cloud of negative energy with him, frightening visitors, and wrecking havoc on the gravestones nearby. While police and grounds people blame teenagers of the broken headstones that occur periodically in the area around the tomb, more then one person has made the connection that they seem to get broken just after someone reports coming in contact with the ghost of an old man in the cemetery. If you visit Valley Street Cemetery today, you will find only oversized, sturdy gravestone markers have survived in the area immediately around the Frederick Smyth mausoleum; all the smaller, more modest tombstones are gone.

Most people who have had contact with this spirit describe a sharp blast of frigid, nearly Antarctic air. They feel pinches and slaps to their arms, even when there is no one there. Cell phones and watch alarms go off incessantly, or fail to work altogether. Some people have said that they even just *feel* tenser when they walk near the tomb, as if they inadvertently had just walked into a room where two people were fighting. Coming in contact with this ghost is like getting an instant adrenaline rush, and fight or flight responses usually kick in quickly.

Whomever the young woman is, she fearful of this negative spirit, and feels she has a duty to keep the living away from him. No one is sure who the two spirits are, or if they could have known each other in life. Is the young woman just trying to keep the negative spirit calm to protect her cemetery from damage? Or does this malignant old ghost have some kind of ill will towards the living that she feels bound to keep in check?

The Aretas Blood Family Tomb, surrounded by fencing as it and the gravestones surrounding it go through restoration.

Raven Duclos and her group of ghost hunters decided to investigate the stories that had been circulating about Valley Street Cemetery. They have visited the grounds several times over the years. Armed with tape recorders and cameras, they have gathered much evidence of the haunting, although they also have been unable to figure out who these spirits are. Interestingly, the avowed psychic and professional ghost hunter describe the place as melancholy, even though the cemetery is a sunny spot in the center of a noisy medium-sized city. Any air of sadness she feels surrounding the place must come from the psychic vibrations of the grounds.

She also describes it as being very haunted. During one of her first trips to Valley Street Cemetery, she felt drawn to the Smyth Mausoleum and, along with several other ghost hunters, decided to take some pictures. Things went along pretty uneventfully until, just as they were talking about where to go next, Raven heard a young woman start screaming at her to get away from the door. She stepped back from the Smyth Mausoleum quickly and called to the others to see if they had heard the shouting, or knew who was warning her away. Somehow no one else had heard the noise. However, when they returned to their office and replayed their tapes, a young woman's voice could be heard, quietly, but quite clearly word for word just as Raven had said.

The back of the infamous Smyth Tomb, which is the center of some un-usual paranormal activity. The front of this mausoleum faces straight out over a thirty-foot drop overlooking the rest of the cemetery.

A few days later, unable to get the experience out of her head, Raven went back to Valley Street. This time she didn't hear anything inexplicable, but several tombstones directly around the Smyth mausoleum were knocked over, and some were cracked right in half. Were they just the work of more teenage vandals? Or were they the work of something much more sinister?

You don't have to be a psychic to experience the ghosts at Valley Street Cemetery. Many average, everyday people, who have never experienced a haunting before, have had strange and unexplainable encounters while on the grounds. It's normal at Valley Street to walk through cold spots on an otherwise sweltering day, feel invisible hands guide you along pathways that no longer exist, or hear whispering voices, even when you are all alone.

Right:
The historic Gale Family mausoleum
at Valley Street
Cemetery.

Flora family marker at Valley Street Cemetery.

Ann is an amateur photographer who lives just outside of Manchester. One day in late spring, she brought her camera equipment with her and decided to take some pictures of the restoration projects going on in the cemetery. Looking at the screen on her digital camera, she saw an old tombstone she wanted to photograph. During that brief hesitation between the time she clicked the digital camera button, and when the camera actually took the picture, she saw very clearly a woman standing behind the marker, resting her hands along the top. Ann looked up, irritated, to ask the woman to leave. But there was no one in sight. When she checked the picture she had taken there was no woman there, but the picture had a bright spot of light obliterating the image altogether. Even though she had been using a digital camera, the image came out over-exposed and useless. Every other picture she took that day came out fine, and her camera has never repeated the bright spot in any other picture.

Some people hope that when the restoration work at Valley Street Cemetery is finished, which is not expected for several more years, that the ghosts who live there will quiet down and be more at peace. However, the cemetery's long history of ghostly phenomena seems to indicate that it will take much more then the planting of some flowerbeds and pruning of trees to make the dead lie easier.

Haunted New Hampshire

Of course, Manchester is not the only haunted place in New Hampshire. There are a great many ghosts and other unexplainable happenings in the areas near the city. Here is a quick look at some of the more famous hauntings in the state that are a comfortable day trip from Manchester.

Concord

Margaritas Mexican Restaurant

This popular bar and restaurant was formerly used as a jail. They even have a few cells left, in case the customers get rowdy! The staff here reports hearing people talking when no one is near them and table decorations getting moved around or hidden. Sometimes, even plates of food move from one place to another. Regulars refer to the ghost as George; he is said to be a prisoner that hung himself in one of the cells.

Old State Mental Hospital

Elevators start up on their own, papers shuffle with no one touching them, heavy footsteps pace the hallways. Sometimes you'll hear the sound of shattering glass, but never find anything broken that could have been the cause of the noise.

Siam Orchid Thai Restaurant

Drinking glasses move across table by themselves and angry voices can be heard fighting in the kitchen of this restaurant—even when there is no one there! The upstairs tenants say they hear a lot of noise coming from the eating establishment, long after everyone has gone home for the night, and doors locked behind them.

Hampton

Island Path Road

In the late 1600s, New England was in the midst of a witch-hunting frenzy. An old woman who lived on what is now Island Path Road became the target for some paranoid townspeople. A group of sea men came to her house one day to taunt her with their accusations. Fed up, she cursed them on the spot. All the men would die later that day when their ship was lost in a storm near the Isles of Shoals. The old woman wasn't executed for their crimes, but she was convicted of witchcraft against the men. She died a few years later, and, over the years, her bones have been moved many times. She haunts Island path Road, upset at the treatment of her body.

Marston House

This house is haunted by an eleven-year-old boy, in a sailor suit, who was accidentally shot and killed while hunting in 1890.

Moulton House

It has long been rumored that the original owner of the house, General Jonathan Moulton, sold his soul to the Devil. But it looks like his wife is the one who is paying the price. Abigail Moulton haunts the 1700s farmhouse where she lived with her husband. Shortly after she died, her husband remarried and gave the young new bride all of Abigail's jewelry. Her ghost appeared that night, presumably to claim her property back from the new wife.

Hollis

Pine Hill Cemetery

This graveyard is more commonly known as the Blood Cemetery, so named because several members of the Blood family, one of Manchester's founding families, are buried here. Abel Blood is also one of the famous ghosts that stalk this plot of land. It is said that, late at night, his headstone changes so the hand pointing heavenward turns upside down, pointing to Hell.

Isles of Shoals

Isles of Shoals are a collection of nine small islands, located just ten miles out to sea, east of Portsmouth, New Hampshire. In the old days, they were sometimes referred to as a shipwreck hotspot, and there are several stories of ghost ships that sail between the islands. Most of the Islands themselves also have many legends about their own personal ghosts.

Lunging Island

Blackbeard and one of his unfortunate wives are said to haunt this island. She may be waiting for her husband to return, and she talks to the people that she comes across. Blackbeard avoids the spirit of his wife as he roams the small island either looking for, or guarding, a treasure chest he is said to have buried here while he was alive.

Star Island
A ghost lives in the Oceanic hotel, sticking mainly to the third and fourth floors. Most often, he is heard moving furniture or pawing through guests' luggage. Dresser drawers open on their own.

White Island
This island has several ghosts. It contains another of Blackbeard's wives, a spirit that roams around Moody's Cave, wailing like a banshee and searching for her lost baby.

Laconia

The Colonial Theater
People have reported the ghostly sounds of people running back and forth along the aisles and hearing voices and screams from all over the building. There are certain seats in the theater that are always cold, even when the air conditioner isn't running.

Old Streetcar Place

This former car factory is now used as office and retail space. The second floor, in particular, seems to be a hotbed of paranormal activity. Along with the sounds of footsteps and faint murmurings, telephones ring constantly, but only static is ever on the other end of the phone. Doors open and slam shut by unseen hands.

Litchfield

Roy Memorial Park

Visitors to the park report seeing a small boy in the cold waters of Darrah Pond asking for help. He disappears when someone enters the water to save him.

Griffin Memorial School

The ghost of a young boy who, legend says, hung himself on the baseball field at Griffin Memorial School, walks around the property on clear nights. Janitors say they also hear desks and chairs moving around at night in the school. In the morning, they find the furniture rearranged into a circular pattern.

Milford

The Burns House

A little girl is seen in the upstairs window of this abandoned house. Several different people, throughout the years, have captured the image of this ghost on film. She seems to be beckoning the photographers to come inside.

Lorden Plaza

A man dressed in blue jeans and a flannel shirt sometimes walks around the plaza, and sometimes, the same figure is seen walking through solid walls! The ghost is only seen outside on the sidewalks, never inside any of the shops.

Monson Center

This is an actual Granite State ghost town! All that remains of the small village is one half-collapsed colonial house, half a dozen cellar holes, and a small graveyard which is suppose to be haunted by spirits who are angry at having been forgotten.

Unitarian Universalist Church

This lovely old Church has a plethora of ghostly activity. Pictures of dozens of orbs have been taken in the basement, the figure of a man sometimes materializes near the stairs, and there is a stationary cold spot in front of one of the doors.

Nashua

Country Tavern

This is one of the more well known New Hampshire hauntings; this ghost seems to be particularly active. It is said to be a former owner of the Tavern, Elizabeth Ford, who was killed by her husband and buried on the grounds.

Gilson Road Cemetery

Transparent figures of ghosts are a common occurrence in this graveyard; it appears to be haunted by many, many ghosts. There are even reports of a malevolent male ghost, dressed in a black robe, that walks through the cemetery at night keeping out intruders. Voices can be heard from the graves at the back of the cemetery. The homes around this cemetery also report many hauntings—cold spots, breaking glass, animals that refuse to enter certain rooms.

Indian Rock Road

This stretch of road a few miles away from Pine Road Cemetery is well traveled by spirits. People walking by report sudden cold spots and the feeling that they're being watched or forced to leave the area.

Portsmouth

The Chase House

This house in Portsmouth has all the ghostly children you'd expect in a former orphanage. Aside from the materialization of these spirits, locked doors suddenly unlock themselves, or vice versa, footsteps are heard wandering around the empty third floor, and the lights and fans in the kitchen turn themselves on and off at will.

Portsmouth Public Library

There are at least three ghosts that are reported to have taken up residence in the downtown library. One is a child who haunts the upper floor, and is most often seen looking down from the second-floor balcony. There is a very modernly dressed ghost that wanders around the building, disregarding annoyances that the living patrons of the library have to walk around, like walls and carts full of library books. The third ghost must be one of the former librarians; it has taken upon itself the job of walking around the library and shushing anyone who gets too rowdy. He is most often seen in the Special Collections Room at the library.

Sheafe Street

The house that stands at this location on Sheafe Street was, for many years, a bed and breakfast, and the ghost that dwells here was a troublesome one to guests and the owners of the building. The ghost would awaken guests in the middle of the night, assaulting them with the strong smell of onions and loud crashes as he threw furniture around. In calmer moments, he endlessly passes back and forth through the hallways, seemingly taking a lot of glee in making his footsteps as loud and obnoxious as possible.

South Cemetery

Two little girls, who were murdered on the Isles of Shoals back in the 1800s, were buried in this cemetery. They manifest in photographs, and pull at the clothes and purses of people who visit the graveyard.

Strawberry Banke

There are several buildings on the grounds of this historical museum and they all seem to have at least one ghost in residence. The most active of these is the Lady in Gray at the Sherburne House.

Salem

Americas Stonehenge

While this attraction isn't actually haunted, it's unusual enough to earn a place in this book. Like the more famous Stonehenge in England, America's Stonehenge is an accurate astronomical calendar. Also like the rock formation in England, we don't know who built it, or how. It is probably the oldest man-made structure in the United States, coming in at just over 4,000 years old.

A Conversation with Manchester's Ghost Hunters

G host Quest is a paranormal research organization that operates out of Manchester
and was founded by acclaimed local psychic Raven Duclos. They have investigated dozens of
haunted houses and mysterious places in Manchester and the surrounding area since they began their
organization in 2003. Their goal is to document and
gather evidence of life after death. They have in their
possession an impressive, and mind boggling, collection of spirit photographs and electronic voice phenomena (EVPs). In some cases, they have also cleared
houses of the spirits lingering there, when the living
owners have been unable to come to terms with their
unwanted ghostly roommates.

Ghost Quest allows guests to come with them on
their research trips, and I was lucky enough to be invited along with them on some of these investigations.
Their leader, Raven Duclos, is probably as close to an
authority on local hauntings, and ghosts in general,
as anyone you are ever likely to meet. She was nice
enough to share many of her experiences with me to
add to this book, and also let me ask her some questions about what it's like tracking down the things that
go bump in the night.

Give us some background on Ghost Quest. How'd the group get started and why?

I have been working as a professional medium for five years, and Ghost Quest came into being three years ago. We, Rebecca Tolley, myself, Doug Warren, Christine and Zane Aikens, began it out of a deep-seated love for anything spiritual. Members have changed over the years and now we have four members—myself, Beckah Boyd (Rebecca Tolley) Katie Boyd and Fred Turner. As said, we all had a love of ghosts and anything spiritual. I have had experiences since my youth, and the thought of having things validated really entrances me.

I believe I've heard that your father was a medium. Do you think that your talents as a psychic are something hereditary that was passed down to you, or do you think that all people have these skills and most just aren't aware of it?

It wasn't my father, it was my grandmother, and yes, I believe some of it is inherited and some of it is inherent. Everyone has abilities. It's a matter of tapping into them. I often liken psychic abilities to that of a piano player. Some people are concert pianists, others can play chopsticks, but with time and learning, anyone can play piano exceedingly well. It's the same for any other talent—including psychic abilities.

There seems to be a lot of different opinions among parapsychologists as to what spirits actually are. In your experience with ghostly phenomena, what do you think people are experiencing, left over psychic energy? The spirits of the dead?

From what I understand, ghosts are mostly people who:

a) linger because they can't accept their death or the circumstances of it,
b) want or need attention,
c) have a heart connection to a place or thing, and choose not to leave, or
d) have an emotional attachment to a person within the place.

There are other types of manifestations. These can be negative or very positive forces that interact with the living.

Is there such a thing as a typical haunting? What are some of the signs that you may be in a haunted house?

I don't believe any haunting is typical, although there are some similarities. The lighter hauntings consist of things being moved, electronic appliances being manipulated, phone calls that have odd numbers (such as birth dates or 000-000-0000), smells that come from nowhere, voices being heard, or foot-

*steps. A heavier haunting would be a lot of sounds,
things being thrown, feelings of threat, fighting in
the home, people being thrown, lifted, or touched in a
hard way such as choking or scratches.*

*What most people don't realize, is that practically
everyone lives in a haunted house— whether it's
spirits coming through, or people we love watching
over us. Most spirits make themselves known because
there is someone in the house they believe can hear
them psychically.*

**Tell us about the kind of people that call you to
investigate their homes.**

*Again, like a haunting, there is no typical person
who calls. But if I had to narrow it down, I would
say they are people who are having pronounced problems due to the
activity in the house. These people call mostly to
get the house cleared, which we do.*

**Walk us through an investigation and tell us
about some of the tools you use. Some one calls because they think their house is haunted, what hap-
pens next?**

*We talk to the person to get an idea of what they
are experiencing; then we go out to the house and
investigate and see what kind of spirit we are dealing
with. We get digital and audio evidence and present
it, then see what the client wants done. If they want*

the spirit cleared, we do that, and then follow up in about a week.

Our tools are basic because, well, none of us are rich. (She laughs.) *We use a medium, a demonologist, an energy reader, a cassette tape recorder, and a digital camera. We utilize other tools as they are available to us.*

What about Manchester in particular? What about the hauntings there?

In Manchester, we have investigated about twenty homes, and no, it is no more or less haunted than any other city or town. But it is wonderfully haunted by some real characters.

Tell us about the most remarkable case you've ever handled in the city.

The most remarkable case we have done in Manchester is a building on Lake Street. It is a three-story building that, at one time, was a gentleman's club. We went during the day to do an investigation and we weren't disappointed. The energies in the place were chaotic, and most of the ghosts were afraid of being made to leave. For evidence, we got picture orbs sitting on a piano that was left on the second floor; combine this with the EVPs that we got of a piano playing. It was very cool; we got pictures of a beastie in the second floor window, of millions of orbs on the third floor.

When we went back at night, the energies were higher. We got a picture of a man leading Beckah up the stairs, but at the time, there was no man there. Beckah also had an extensive channeling session with a woman named Joan. I felt like I was going to have a heart attack because of three ghosts that sur- rounded me, and when I got downstairs and cleared with the help of Katie, we got pictures of them. It was incredible.

Ravens group, Ghost Quest, can be found online at www.ghostquest.org. On their site, you will find the results of many of their investigations, as well as some of the spirit photographs and some chilling audiotape EVPs of voices from beyond the grave. You can reach them to have them investigate your haunted house, for free, through the website, and get information about joining them as a guest or member.

Spirit Photography 101

For most ghost hunters, professionals, and hobbyists alike, the real thrill is in getting proof of life after death—something that would make even the most staunch skeptics change their positions on the subject. For some people, this means bringing along a tape recorder and trying to get audio proof of hauntings. An audio recorder is one of the basic tools that ghost hunters usually bring on an investigation, and even though they may hear nothing ghostly while they are onsite, after playing back the tape, you sometimes hear hushed voices faintly speaking. However, some experts in the paranormal are skeptical of electronic voice phenomena, and others think it may be a downright dangerous thing for amateurs to try.

The safest, easiest, way to bring back a souvenir of your haunted experienced is with a piece of equipment you probably already own—a camera. A regular 35 mm camera works just fine; you don't need special film or anything! Digital cameras seem to have even better luck picking up unexplainable anomalies, but some people have questioned how reliable they are.

It's your call; find the camera that feels best in your hands, and stick with it. You may take a lot of photos before finding anything strange caught on film, but if you persevere, the law of averages are on your side, and you'll pick up something eventually.

Here are some tips and tricks to help you improve your chances of capturing the image of life after death.

Always carry a camera with you. The more time you spend learning about hauntings, the more sensitive you become to presences. Always have a camera on you, just in case. Go buy a bargain pack of disposable cameras, keep one in your glove compartment of your car, one in your purse or on your person, one at work, etc.

Trust your instincts. The majority of ghost photographs aren't even discovered until you develop your film. Remember, just because you don't see something right in front of you with the naked eye, doesn't mean there's nothing there. If you get the feeling you should snap a picture of something, do it, even if you can't explain why you had the feeling.

Bring a friend. One of the best ways to prove that you caught something strange on film is to show the same anomaly at the same time, but on another person's camera.

Take your time. Experts seem to agree that the best time to start taking photos is a half hour *after* you get to the site.

Keep away from the light. Watch out for reflections from the bright sun, particularly full moons, your camera flash reflecting off televisions, shiny polished floors, street lights, and about ten dozen other things I'm sure you can think of. Many people mistake these things for evidence as ghosts, and are sadly disappointed when they find out the occurrence has a perfectly average explanation.

Bring a thermometer. A compass works well, too, but a thermometer is easy for anyone to use and most people already have at least one. Keep your eye on the thermometer as you walk around—a sudden, unexplainable drop in the temperature is your clue to start clicking!

Be realistic. No matter how many you see online, full-body shots of a transparent figure are very rare in ghost photography. Although it does happen, don't get your hopes quite that high. The most common types of ghost photographs are called orbs. These look like fuzzy balls, usually a whitish gray, although more colorful ones aren't unheard of.

Always be honest. There is a certain amount of competitiveness between ghost hunters. Some people just starting out might feel a great deal of pressure to come up with a ghost photograph. Never fake a ghost picture, even if it's just as a joke to show your friends. Most of the time, an experienced ghost hunter can tell when something has been faked, and faking phenomena just gives skeptics more ammunition in their crusades against the occult. Give it time and you'll get the photo you want.

The most important thing to remember is to relax, have fun, and be safe. Always ask permission before entering a haunted house, or make sure that where you are going isn't about to collapse on top of you. It's important to get permission before going onto private property. Remember, ghost photography is still much more an art than a science.

These tips can help make it more likely that you'll get a good picture, but there are no guarantees. If you have trouble getting any kind of anomalies at one haunted house, try going at a different time of day, or a different spot in that area.

Like many things involving the afterlife, there are as many proponents of ghost photography and other kinds of ghostly occurrences as there are those debunking the notions.

The truth is that, as technologically advanced as we've become, science still doesn't have all the answers. There are still a great many mysteries left in life, and in death. Does something of a person's personality live on after the body has died? Are ghosts real, or part of our imaginations?

Whether you decide to try ghost hunting yourself and attempt to get "proof" of life after death, or just enjoy reading about other peoples' ghostly encounters in books (like this one!), ultimately, in the end, it's up to you to decide. What do *you* believe? Are there ghosts?

Bibliography
and Website Resources

The following books and websites were essential towards the research for *Manchester Ghosts*. If you're looking for more information on ghosts, hauntings, or the history of New Hampshire's Queen City these are excellent places to start.

Benway, Katie. "Ghost Jogger". *Hippo Press* (October 25, 2001).

Blackman, W. Haden. *The Field Guide to North American Hauntings: Everything You Need to Know About Encountering Over 100 Ghosts, Phantoms, and Spectral Entities.* New York, New York: Three Rivers Press, 1998.

Citro, Joseph A. *Weird New England: Your Travel Guide to New England's Local Legends and Best Kept Secrets.* New York, New York: Sterling Publishing Company, 2005.

Clayton, John. "In the City". *The Union leader* (May 1, 1995).

Dole, Jennifer. "Hessers Hauntings". *Hippo Press.* (October 25, 2001).

Forrest, Jim. "Rock Rimmon Has Spawned Many Legends". *The Journal* (March 18, 1981).

Hayward, Mark. "West Side Neighbors Rally 'Round 'Rock". *The Union Leader* (July 16, 2001).

Jolly, Martyn. *Faces of the Living Dead: The Belief in Spirit Photography.* New York, New York: Mark Batty Publisher, 2006.

Lamb, Fred W. "Old Timer". *The Amoskeag Bulletin* (July 1, 1914).

Manning, Erin. "Whispers, Rumors, Legends, and Stuff We Heard". *Hippo Press* (October 25, 2001).

Southall, Richard. *How to be a Ghost Hunter.* Saint Paul,
   Minnesota: Llewellyn Publications, 2003.

Thorpe, L.Ashton. *Manchester of Yesterday.* Manchester,
   New Hampshire: Granite State Press, 1939.

Author not credited. "Rock Rimmon Rescue". *The
   Union Leader* (August 4, 1992).

Author not credited. "There's Some Good Haunting
   in New Hampshire". *New Hampshire Sunday News*
   (October 27, 1996).

Website Resources:

   www.GhostQuest.org
   www.GhostTowns.com
   www.GhostVillage.com
   www.HollowHill.com
   www.ManchesterNH.gov
   www.NewEnglandGhosts.com
   www.NewHampshire.com
   www.NHGraveyards.org
   www.NH.Searchroots.com
   www.Valley-Cemetary.com